From These Green Heights

From These Green Heights was commissioned by the Axis Art Centre, Ballymun, and first staged by them in Ballymun, Dublin, Ireland on 24 November 2004, directed by Ray Yeates.

CAST
(In order of appearance)
Dessie: Alan King
Christy: Vincent McCabe
Carmel: Anne Kent
Marie: Melanie Grace
Jane: Ann O'Neill
Tara: Doireann Ní Chorragain
Sharon: Catherine Barry
Junkie: Karen Brady

PRODUCTION
Director: Ray Yeates
Set & Costume Designer: Marie Tierney
Design Associate: Robert Ballagh
Lighting: Conleth White
           Sarah Kivlehan
Music: Mark O'Brien
Producer: Roisin McGarr
Stage Manager: Jackie Dwyer
Assistant Stage Manager: David Gilna
Sound Operator: James O'Neill

From These Green Heights

Dermot Bolger

NEW
ISLAND

FROM THESE GREEN HEIGHTS
First published 2005
by New Island
2 Brookside
Dundrum Road
Dublin 14
www.newisland.ie

ISBN 1 904301 85 1

British Library Cataloguing in Publication Data. A CIP catalogue record for this book is available
from the British Library.

Typeset by New Island
Cover photograph taken by Eamonn Elliott and designed by Form, illustrated by Eleanor
McCaughey. Produced courtesy of Axis Art Centre, Ballymun.
Printed by J.H.Haynes & Co. Ltd, Sparkford

New Island received financial assistance from
The Arts Council (An Chomhairle Ealaíon), Dublin, Ireland.

the arts
council
chomhairle
ealaíon

10 9 8 7 6 5 4 3 2 1

For Emile Jean Dumay and Ray Yeates,
both of whom inspired me to write for the stage again

Characters
(between six and eight)

Dessie – *a man in his forties*
Christy – *Dessie's father*
Carmel – *Dessie's mother*
Marie – *Dessie's partner*
Jane – *Marie's mother*
Tara* – *ten-year-old daughter of* **Dessie** *and* **Marie**
Sharon* - *late teens/early twenties – sister of* **Marie**
Junkie* – *mid-twenties.*

*In productions where it proves financially impossible to employ such a large cast it is possible for one actress to play all three parts.

Time
1966–2004

The play should exist in one continuous motion with no scene breaks.

ACT ONE

Half-light comes up. Most of the stage is divided into three raked and interconnecting ramps positioned at slightly different heights to allow the cast to move easily from one to the other. The cast can also sit at the front or back of these ramps and may also use the remaining stage space in front of them. Alternative settings may be used once overt literalness is avoided. Beyond the edge of the ramps, to stage left and right, there is a row of chairs facing across from each other so that those members of cast not involved in the action at any particular time can sit here, engaged in observing what is occurring on stage. In this way, the cast almost serve as the play's internal audience, listening to and silently supporting each other's stories with their presence. There is no distinction between the living and the dead. In this initial half-light the entire cast line the backdrop (a towering, abstract representation of the tower blocks) except for the **Junkie** *who crosses to stand on the bare stage beyond the ramps at the front.*

Junkie   Whose voice can you hear?
Who's calling down the stair?
What ghost trapped in a lift-shaft?
What child who played and laughed?

Every touch and every trust and every kiss,
Every feud, every fight, every lip split,
Every face lost at the window of a tower block,
Every loan shark with a list of women in hock.

Every whiskey, every Valium, every cigarette,
Every couple holding hands in a kitchenette,
Every laughing child being spun in the August sun,
Every boy with a piebald horse to gallop on.

Why won't the voices stop whispering,
Straining to be heard amid the babbling?
Lives that were ended and lives begun,
The living and the dead of Ballymun.

*The **Junkie** and the rest of the cast file off to the seats, left and right, as lights raise and **Dessie** comes forward, placing a suitcase down before walking to the bare stage at the front. His parents, **Christy** and **Carmel**, each stand on a ramp to the left and right of him, apart and yet both towering protectively over him due to the raised rake.*

Dessie   England won the World Cup that year, which annoyed both my da and Denis Law. I don't remember it, being only five years of age. But I've a memory of setting out one Sunday afternoon. Ma making heaps of sandwiches in the kitchenette of our cramped flat in Bolton Street in town like we were venturing to the furthest reaches of Mongolia or Meath. Da coming in from writing a letter for a neighbour, lifting me up onto the table to laugh about the brand new home I'd see being built like a rocket in the sky. We weren't just moving up in the world – we were moving skyward. The word struck me, because I thought it was two words, sky and wood. I don't know what I imagined, maybe a green orchard suspended at that height amid the clouds, a nesting place for Da's pigeons, a woodland where I could reach from my bedroom window to pluck the fruit glistening there. I just know that we waited for a bus, then we walked …

Christy (*steps forward to stand beside the suitcase, behind* **Dessie**, *close but not touching*)   … and walked and bloody well walked, miles past the Albert College out into uncharted territory. To be honest I knew the general terrain better than I let on, from my courting days when I bore an uncanny resemblance to Johnny Weissmuller, the Olympic swimmer who exposed more than his chest swinging between trees in the Tarzan films. I'd often cycled out that way with a mot on my crossbar, seeking a bit of privacy for our explorations. However, I could hardly confess those particular natural history lessons to my missus. A few bewildered locals hung about that Sunday, lured from their cottages near Dubber Cross by the promise of jobs at the new Balency pre-cast on-site factory. Bogmen on black bicycles, with flecks of dandruff on their black suits just to add a touch of colour. Gaping at the tower blocks appearing in their fields like they were alien spacecraft adorned with Dublin Corporation signs picked up in some intergalactic sale of work.

Dessie   There were crowds from Finglas and Santry and disgruntled residents from nearby private estates like

Pinewood muttering about blow-ins, even though the
foundations were barely set on their own houses. It felt
strange knowing no one, when I was used to playing in a
protective shoal of older boys. Maybe it was because I'd
never known how vast the world was, but ...

Christy ... and I couldn't let on before the missus, but
... I was scared by the newness of everything.

Dessie *and* **Christy** *both turn to look at* **Carmel** *to their left
as she speaks, yet all three keep their own separate space.*

Carmel I wasn't scared one bit. I was thrilled to be
leaving Bolton Street, having seen firemen carry the
corpses of children from the rubble of a collapsed
tenement there. I'd never felt safe in our two rooms after
that. We hadn't been evacuated like some, but with every
creak on a windy night you'd be waiting for the roof to
collapse in on you. The Minister for Local Government,
Neil Blaney, seemed to me like an overweight Moses with
a bogman's accent, leading my family out here to the
Promised Land. *Ard Glas* – Green Heights – that's what
he first wanted to call it. The Ballymun flats weren't
finished that Sunday we went out here. They still hadn't
laid out the acres of orchards Blaney promised where
children could run at twilight and the playgrounds you
normally only saw in films about New York. No shops
were built yet or clinics or schools. But all these things
were promised and moving to Ballymun seemed almost
as classy as moving to America.

4

Dessie *steps back to the edge of the ramp with* **Christy** *and* **Carmel** *standing together at his shoulder so that all three look up in wonder, as a family group, with* **Dessie**'*s demeanour now that of an awe-struck child.*

Dessie (*tugs at her sleeve*) Which flat will be ours, Ma?

Carmel Don't know yet, Dessie, but they'll all be lovely when it's finished.

Dessie How will your pigeons find their way here, Da?

Christy Sure the Corpo will paint signs on the rooftops in Drumcondra, saying '*Intelligent pigeons this way*'.

Dessie Pigeons can't read, Da.

Christy Who says so? Some folk don't like reading – it gives your mother headaches – but why do you think I line their coop with old copies of the *Dandy*? They're always complaining about you taking so long to read it.

Carmel (*smiles*) We won't know ourselves out here, son.

Christy (*half to himself as* **Dessie** *drifts upstage exploring*) We won't know anyone else, either.

Carmel What's that?

Christy (*hastily*) Just saying I wouldn't know my way

here. I was never beyond Drumcondra in my life ...
courting or ...

Carmel A fellow brought me out here once.

Dessie *sits on the stage, listening.*

Christy What fellow?

Carmel On his bicycle.

Christy Hope he got a bloody puncture.

Carmel Down a lane with a stream at the end and a
woman coming out of a big farmhouse on a pony and
trap and you knew by the tilt of her nose that she was a
Protestant. Swarms of midges under trees and the taste
off the bottle of milk in his jacket that had soured in the
heat.

Christy He'd have better kept his bloody jacket on.

Carmel It was all very innocent. I was sixteen and
working in the sewing factory. A printer's apprentice from
Dominic Street. Are you jealous?

Christy Of someone from Dominic Street? You must be
joking. They're still only getting over the famine in
Dominic Street. He must have stolen the bicycle and

found the jacket on a skip. Wander off to Sillogue Lane on a crossbar with any pauper you want.

Carmel (*teasing*)   I never mentioned the name of the lane.

Christy   Did you not? A lucky guess. (*He embraces her.*) Occasionally in life I get lucky.

Carmel   How lucky?

Christy   The luckiest man alive.

Dessie *watches them move to the edge of the stage, stage left, while* **Tara** *(his ten-year-old daughter) rises from her seat, stage right, and crosses to stage to where* **Dessie** *sits, momentarily having trouble getting his attention.*

Tara   Dad? Mammy says we're to bring the boxes out into the hall. You're doing no work with the pair of us slaving.

Dessie (*looks around, rises*)   I'm coming, Tara, I was just …

Tara   Were Gran and Grandad the first people to live here, Daddy?

Dessie   In this flat or in Ballymun?

Tara In the flat. I mean nobody lived in Ballymun before the flats were built, did they?

Dessie My da once told me that it had a population of thirty-four souls in 1900 sharing eight inhabited buildings. That's not counting the foxes and badgers who ran wild. Their ghosts would get some shock if they saw it now.

Tara (*takes his hand*) But there's no ghosts in this tower block, is there?

Dessie No.

Tara You're not just saying that, Daddy?

Dessie Well, if there is, they can have it to themselves once we finish packing and close over the door tonight.

Tara What will our new home be like?

Dessie (*smiles wryly*) Perfect, like my ma used to say. Just wait until it's finished.

As **Tara** *exits,* **Carmel** *turns around to kneel beside the suitcase, which she opens, and begins to take out vases wrapped in old newspaper.* **Dessie** *has taken a toy car from his jacket pocket and lies down, stage right, playing with it.*

Carmel looks across with good-humoured exasperation as

Christy *observes them.*

Carmel   Are you going to do nothing but stand there dreaming?

Dessie (*puts the toy car away*)   Just looking around, Ma.

Carmel   We've all night to look around once we get moved in. (*To* **Christy**) Did you tip Mr McCarthy for the use of his truck?

Dessie *strays forward and mimes peering over a balcony.*

Christy   I gave him a few bob for a pint, as if he hadn't already bled us dry. We should have charged *him*. He'd more fun riding up and down in that lift, when we could get into it with all the furniture people are carting out here with them. He wants me to write to the Corporation for him about some permit, says my handwriting is as good as a typed letter.

Carmel   Will you?

Christy   I will, for all the good it will do. Still, if you can't help your neighbours, even your ex-neighbours. He knows the Brennans who've moved in across the hall. From Hatch Street. (*To* **Dessie**) Mind yourself on that balcony, Dessie.

Dessie (*thrilled*) You can see the whole world from here.
Where will the orchards be, Mammy?

Christy Orchards? I never met a Corporation workman
who could do more than plant his feet into size twelve
hobnail boots and even that's half a day's work for them.
You'd have more chance of getting orchards by throwing
apple pips out the window.

Dessie *has come over to kneel beside* **Carmel** *and the suitcase.*

Carmel Don't mind him, son. I know it's all a muddy
building site now, but just wait until Ballymun is
finished. We're going to be happy here, (*suddenly anxious*)
aren't we, Christy?

Christy Course we will. Sure we're half-way to paradise
perched up here already. Even my pigeons will get
vertigo. We'll be grand – you, me, Dessie and, in time, a
few more chislers to keep him company. (*Wipes his
forehead*) Holy James Street, but it's warm. Do the
Corporation ever turn the heat off? Hard enough getting
used to radiators without not even having a bloody knob
to twiddle with.

Carmel Sure you wouldn't know how to twiddle with it,
you never saw a radiator in your life. They say it comes
on once the temperature outside drops below sixty
degrees Fahrenheit. Is that hot or cold, Christy?

Christy Don't know, except that it's like living in the banana house in the Botanic Gardens. Maybe the orchards they plan are tropical bloody indoor plantations. I tell you one thing, you're wearing no grass skirt, especially if any neighbours turn out to be printers from Dominic Street.

Dessie *wanders back to playing with his toy car, stage right.*

Carmel You can have a bath tonight.

Christy Sure I've a bath every Friday whether I need it or not.

Carmel You can have one every night without having to lug coal upstairs. Imagine, Christy?

Christy Ah hold on now, a man needs some natural dirt as a protective lining against the elements ...

Carmel *roots in the suitcase to produce an old-fashioned wooden back scrubber, which she tosses at him.*

Carmel (*firmly*) Wash. All over.

Christy (*resigned*) Yes, Mam.

Christy *walks off to sit stage right, followed by* **Carmel** *who leaves the suitcase open and half unpacked as* **Dessie** *rises to become an adult again.*

Dessie   Kids swarming everywhere, banging on doors to see if you wanted to play. It was a great worry to Ma that the ground was so far away. I wasn't allowed down unless with the Brennan boys. The other neighbours were from all over the gaff: Bride Street, Thomas Street, even the Coombe. The Flynns upstairs had been in temporary accommodation since their flat in Fenian Street was condemned. They even once spent a week camped out on the street. You could hear them run baths at midnight for the thrill of it. But generally you heard little because we were all chosen as model tenants. We became best friends with the Brennans. No shite about them, as Da said when he thought I wasn't listening. Not like the McGraths beside us. Ma said they had more airs than Moore's melodies. Their grandfather lived with them, an old stevedore who sat on the balcony all day, even in the rain, because he couldn't stick the dry air inside with no fireplace to spit into. He lived for Sweet Afton and bull's-eyes and died after eight months from a lack of conversation. (**Christy** *rises from his chair.*) The first funeral in our tower block. The lift broke with his coffin stuck inside it and Ma said it wasn't from the weight of his sins anyhow. It was the oddest funeral, Da said, with neighbours trying to be neighbourly. But what could you do except stand around the hearse in the churned-up mud outside the tower where workmen were still laying pipes, then walk a mile to catch a bus into town with the church in Gardiner Street closed before you reached it.

Christy (*stepping onto the stage right as* **Dessie** *drifts across to the left where he turns to observe him*) The McGraths complained to the Housing Welfare Department about my pigeons. A Corpo official called in, a pigeon fancier himself. Said he'd have to file a complaint, then winked and mentioned a race from Wales that he was putting two birds in for. My pigeons needed a run but so far I'd entered them in nothing. Don't know why. They were no champions, just a poor strain of half-breeds … like Kildare people. A true racing man would wring their necks and start again. But my pigeons were like me, slow and uneasy with change. I didn't find Ballymun easy, to be honest, fighting my way onto a bus every day after work in the joinery in Francis Street, barely able to see out through the cigarette smoke. There was something bleak about Ballymun. It seemed mad to move people into what was still a building site, where even the buses had to stop a mile away because they couldn't get through the mud. The consortium due to build the shopping centre took one look at us and seemed in no hurry to take a second one. Or maybe they had a franchise on the little van shops springing up. All the same I knew that it was time to let my pigeons go.

Dessie (*childish voice*) Will the pigeons not hate being on the boat to Wales, Da?

Christy They travel first class, each with their own steel cabin. (*Turns from* **Dessie**) They would long for the traps to open to join the mass of feathers unfurling in the air as each one found its path home. Home was the all-important word. The pigeons were my lie detector, sharing feelings I couldn't express. Would Ballymun ever feel like home? Three months after we moved in Carmel miscarried. Ten weeks gone. Conceived in the first flush of arrival. The Ballymun baby we'd called it. I'd have blamed all the baths, only she miscarried twice before. But this third miscarriage was hard, with no one around that Carmel knew to talk to. Still it hadn't stopped us trying and this time the news was good. Twenty weeks gone but I was on edge and somehow the baby had got wrapped up in my mind with the pigeons. This flat wouldn't feel like home until it was filled with kids' voices, and I felt sure the pigeons wouldn't return if barren times lay ahead because their instincts never lied. That Saturday I sat out on the balcony with my field glasses long before the race leaders crossed the Irish Sea. Time dragged past and I was convinced they'd gone to Bolton Street, flying in and out of broken windows there, roosting amid the rafters and the mice. Then at last a speck came amongst the other specks in the sky and I knew in my soul that it was one of my birds and everything would be all right. (*Holds out his hands, drawing in an imaginary bird*) Snowball landed, a bit suspicious, then walked into my hands. Carmel and Dessie came out.

Carmel *rises from her seat to join him on stage with* **Dessie** — *as a child — also approaching to complete the family group.*

Carmel She's home …

Christy Never any doubt. (*Holds the imaginary bird in one hand and with the other hand places* **Dessie**'s *fingers on* **Carmel**'s *stomach*) What do you say, Dessie, will it be a boy or a child?

Dessie A sister, but how will she get out of Ma's tummy?

Christy I can tell you scientifically.

Carmel Christy! If my mother knew that he knows half of what he already knows.

Christy Ballymun is a New World, love. No more cabbage leaves and superstition. Do you know how she'll come out, son? Roaring and screaming for her bottle. (*Hands* **Dessie** *an unseen ring*) Enter Snowball's time on the clock, son, there might be a prize for last.

Christy *and* **Carmel** *retake their seats, leaving* **Dessie** *sitting on the back edge of the ramp, staring away from the audience as* **Marie** (**Dessie**'s *wife*) *enters to kneel beside the suitcase, beginning to pack away the same possessions that* **Carmel** *has previously unpacked.* **Tara** *enters, holding a racing clock, and kneels beside* **Marie**.

Tara What's this, Mammy?

Marie (*takes it*)   God, does your father throw anything out? A racing clock, from when your father's father kept pigeons.

Tara   Did your father keep pigeons?

Marie (*packing away the clock in the suitcase*)   My father would have thought himself above pigeons. Bit of a snob. Used to sign cheques Derek Farrell, B.A.

Tara   What does B.A. stand for?

Marie   Bad apple.

Tara   Will I call Dad again?

Marie   Leave him, pet. Are you excited?

Tara   A bit scared, Mammy. What if I don't like the new house in Poppintree?

Marie   That's the chance you take. Life is full of chances, the spin of a coin.

Tara   What do you mean?

Marie   I saw good and bad things growing up here. It makes you realise how every new day is a miracle.

Tara   Am I a miracle?

16

Marie (*snapping the packed suitcase shut*)   The most precious one. Give me a hand or we'll never get packed.

They exit left with the suitcase as **Dessie** *turns to look at the audience.*

Dessie   I woke and knew something was wrong. It wasn't any noise because even the lift shaft was silent. It was like the air was solid around the tower block with night birds frozen in mid flight. We were eighteen months half here. Then my bedroom door opened and Da picked me up in my pyjamas and said to be a brave little boy, carrying me out with my eyes sore from sleep. The sour feeling in my stomach …

Carmel (*still seated, stage right, beside* **Christy**)   And Dessie's little hands balled up to his eyes. I wanted to hold him but was afraid. I had my arms pressed against my womb because I knew I was losing the baby in that unnatural pain and she was dying with part of me dying too. Not due for another seven weeks. I wanted to scream but I couldn't because Dessie looked so scared …

Christy (*seated*) … when I handed him to Mrs Brennan to place him in the bed among her own lads. And I asked Mr Brennan again if he minded driving and he said to talk sense, man. Then we found that some little prick must have vandalised the bloody lifts, because they had worked a few hours before. So we walked down through the night.

They rise and, with difficulty, step up onto the stage, **Christy** *supporting* **Carmel** *as they take a few steps across it.*

Carmel   Every step torture, feeling the baby slip away amid the pain and praying I would not have to lie down and miscarry on these concrete stairs. I longed to be back in Bolton Street, with women I knew on each landing. Two youths stood on waste ground outside the tower and I realised that this was what it was – waste ground. No orchards were being planted for my daughter to run in. (*She slips onto her knees*) And then in the back of Mr Brennan's Ford Anglia all hope gave way inside me as we drove past the unbuilt shops and vacant spaces and I screamed at the blood I was covered in. Neither man spoke on the way to hospital because what was there to say …

Carmel *rises and exits, leaving* **Christy** *alone.*

Christy   … except that I wanted to kill the little bastard who broke the lift and I wanted to hold my wife and tell her how I had gone to bed still a young man and woke to find myself cast adrift in middle age.

Dessie (*rises from the back of the stage to approach* **Christy**) Next morning the Brennan boys were sent to the mobile van to buy sausages for my breakfast, but I just longed for Ma and Da to come back. Only Da came to say how Ma was in hospital and my unborn sister was in paradise, a hundred floors up, where they really had tropical orchards with pigeons flying amid the green heights. Her unbaptised soul was not stuck in some halfway Limbo. Da's voice sounded older.

Christy   Because Limbo is for the living, son, not for the dead.

Christy *sits at the front edge of the stage right while* **Dessie** *exits and* **Marie** *enters from stage left.*

Marie   My kid sister Sharon wanted to be a limbo dancer. We saw them once at Fossetts Circus in Whitehall. Don't know where Mam found the money. Me? I wanted to go to Australia or become a dental assistant. The careers brochure said you needed clean hands and the Inter Cert. The summer I turned fourteen I got a job sweeping up in a ladies' salon on Glasnevin Avenue. I mentioned my dream to a customer from a private house on Willow Park who suggested that hairdressing would suit me better. It took me a minute to realise why. She could tolerate someone from the flats touching her hair, but hated the notion that my fingers might come in contact with her mouth. Dental assistants don't do that. You wear a class of nurse's uniform and smile to reassure people as they sit down. It's like being an airhostess only without the chance to meet pilots, unless they need an extraction. I used to love Mills and Boon books, all those Sebastians and Ricks falling for

Annabels and Tiffanys. Mills and Boon heroines were
never named after Catholic saints and the heroes are
never dentists. Still, at the age of eleven I became a
realist. Life changed and I would never be courted by
young doctors parking sports car outside the flats. I
would never toss my hat in the air after graduating from
Trinity College. In Australia, though, I would be free of
this stigma and let nobody say that I couldn't be a dental
assistant in either country. (*She tilts back the chair*) Lie
back and relax, sir, the dentist will attend to you shortly.
Open wider for the needle, just a small prick and you'll
feel nothing. Your dentist's chair is cruising at twenty
thousand feet, we will shortly pass through the cabin
with a pink liquid to rinse out your mouth with. Look to
your left and you will see the Ballymun towers below.
They will take your mind off the tooth being extracted.
Don't fret, at this altitude nobody can hear you scream.
Half a mile to your right you will see Pinewood Crescent
where your immaculately attired dental hostess once lived
in a private house with a father whom the neighbouring
women loved for being so obliging with his hands. You
look quite like him, Rick. Women said my mother was
lucky to have him. Only she rarely had him, as he was
always off tightening something for some lady up the
street with his trusty spanner. Hadn't my mother enough
to do, minding my sister and me? Lie back, Rick, these
other teeth look lonely with their companion gone. What
would you need an anaesthetic for, and you a pilot? Did
you ever wake to voices arguing? Hugging your baby

sister tight, knowing you'd give anything to make the shouting stop. We gave up our house. In 1972 we moved half a mile to the eighth floor of a tower block. Me, Mum, Sharon. There was shouting above us all night, but at least it wasn't my parents. It was squatters who had moved in. Other girls called me a snob. My doll's pram was stolen. Mum found it smashed in an underpass. Daddy disappeared to Coventry. They say he was last seen being dropped from an aeroplane without a parachute, strapped to a dentist's chair.

Marie *exits as* **Christy** *rises.*

Christy We would have called her Mary had she been born alive. The stairs wouldn't have felt steep when I carried down her pram because I would have been using my strength for my daughter. I'd have taught her to have beautiful handwriting. I'd have carried her on my shoulders to the church for her first communion. But what use was strength when I couldn't do these things? People had a new term for what I felt – the high-rise blues. There was a lot of it around, especially among the workers laid off at the factory that had been churning out pre-cast moulds that nobody wanted any more because the experts who came to study us decided that these towers were not, after all, the start of a golden era. Ballymun was a mistake, with the pre-cast workers given their cards because such towers would never be built again. That wasn't the only dream gone. Doctors said that

another pregnancy could put Carmel's life in danger. I
didn't want to take that risk, yet she didn't want to put
her body off limits because we were husband and wife …
scared and in love and scared that our love might cause
her death. I'd to ask men in pubs on the quays going to
England to smuggle home johnnies for me. Having to
laugh at their crude jokes about me having a mot on the
side. And the few times we made love it was an awkward,
careful-not-to-come-too-soon or not-to-come-at-all love,
a cocktail of risk and longing. (*Begins to cross the stage to
the left*) And so that Carmel wouldn't see how I was
hurting I went walking most evenings, past the shopping
centre that was finally being built and the roundabout
where youths gathered in the underpass. One night I saw
a woman kneel there, examining a wrecked doll's pram.
(**Marie** *enters, right, child-like, holding a skipping rope,
watching him*) A good-looking woman crying with stress.
I went to say something but her eyes told me to mind my
own business. I walked past in my private grief and left
her to her own pain.

As **Christy** *exits* **Marie** *begins to skip.*

Marie *(chants)* Cinderella, dressed in yella,
Went upstairs to kiss her fella,
By mistake she kissed a snake,
How many kisses does it take
One, two, three …

Dessie *has crossed the stage, with* **Marie** *regarding him with childish curiosity.*

Dessie (*turns back*) Oi, where'd you get all the freckles?

Marie In a bleeding freckle factory. What's it to you, you're only a kid.

Dessie I'm thirteen in August.

Marie I was thirteen in May. If people saw us talking they'd think me a cradle-snatcher. Why aren't you playing football?

Dessie I'm sick of that game. It's been next-goal-the-winner since last Tuesday.

Marie (*walks over to join him*) Boys are boring. Do you like T-Rex? I hate David Cassidy. All my class love him, but I think if he was a lollipop he'd eat himself.

Dessie My ma never plays music on the radio any more.

Marie What does she do?

Dessie What's it to you? (*Looks around*) Why haven't you any friends of your own?

Marie Why haven't you?

Dessie   I've loads. All into Status Quo. (*Begins miming an air guitar*) Twenty-minute air-guitar solos. My fingers need a rest.

Marie   I see you running some mornings out towards St Margaret's.

Dessie   I like running. It helps me think.

Marie   Maybe I'll overtake you. You'd never catch up.

Dessie   I'd catch you in a minute.

Marie   You wouldn't. A girl with her skirt up runs faster than a boy with his pants down. (*Stops and blushes*) I didn't just say that, did I?

Dessie (*embarrassed*)   I have to ... join the match.

Marie (*mortified*)   Listen ... I didn't mean ... girls in my class they're always telling filthy jokes ... I was just trying to sound as tough ...

Dessie   Yeah ... I have to see the lads.

Marie   What does your mother do? Instead of listening to the radio?

Carmel *rises from her seat to stand on right of stage.*

Dessie (*beat, quiet honesty*)   When she thinks I'm not looking she sometimes cries.

Marie   So does mine.

Self-consciously they exit in different directions as **Christy** *enters from the left, slightly unsteady as he approaches* **Carmel**.

Carmel   You're drunk.

Christy   So what?

Carmel   So it's half eight of a Friday. I've been waiting two hours for you to come home with your dinner burnt.

Christy   I'm not hungry.

Carmel   I cooked it, you can eat it.

Christy   Said I am not hungry.

Carmel   I don't care what you said. I climbed down those bloody stairs to shop for you. My feet are aching, I'm exhausted and I've cooked for you.

Christy   Like a good Catholic wife.

Carmel   What does that mean? These days you hardly ever go near me.

Christy   You know why. I'm scared.

Carmel   Of failure?

Christy (*hurt*)   I'd my share of women before I met you. I had …

Carmel   You had what?

Christy (*embarrassed*)   I'm drunk and talking shite.

Carmel   Maybe you need to be drunk to say the truth. You don't fancy me any more, do you?

Christy   That's not it.

Carmel   What is it then?

Christy   You know who you are. You wash, cook, raise our son well, you've nothing to be ashamed of.

Carmel (*confused*)   What shite are you talking now?

Christy   I'm talking about what I am. I'd a trade that was meant to keep us going for life.

Carmel   Have you a problem in work?

Christy   I've no work to have a problem with. The joinery closed last month. Cheap fucking imports.

Carmel How could it have closed and you never told me?

Christy Because I thought I'd pick up something else. An honest carpenter could always walk into a job in this city. I'd contacts, a whisper in the right ear on the street. But the grapevine doesn't stretch to Ballymun. Who will I meet on a bus out here? I said nothing because between the few bob I'd stashed away and the dole I could put the same money for you on the kitchen table these last few Thursdays. We're not destitute, we're just …

Carmel You never told me.

Christy (*desperate*) You know me, I'm not good at telling people anything beyond old yarns. I thought I'd get settled into another job and then tell you when there'd be no need for alarm … when you wouldn't doubt me …

Carmel I don't doubt you.

Christy Well, you can start because I doubt myself. In and out of factories these last weeks, places I used to work or knew someone who knew someone once. It's amazing the difference between the gaffers who knew me in Bolton Street and those who didn't. The others just hear this address and their minds are already made up. They keep blaming the oil crisis, the three-day week in

Britain, but I don't believe them. You'd swear we were living in fucking Siberia.

Carmel (*quietly*) There's no need to swear.

Christy I've been living a lie. You making me sandwiches at night and me terrified you'd meet someone who knew the truth. But who the hell would you meet out here? All the job adverts I've replied to, scared that you might get Dessie to open the letters that came back and read out the standard brush-offs.

Carmel (*hurt*) I never open your mail, I'm frightened of letters.

Christy I know.

Carmel Besides I wouldn't need Dessie anyway. If I wanted to read them I could make the words out.

Christy I know you could.

Carmel Just never had much cause for reading. Sit down. I'll get your dinner.

Christy You should throw it at me.

Carmel It's so solid now it would leave scars.

Christy I was a fool not to tell you.

Carmel You're a good workman. You'll find something.

Christy Will I?

Carmel Do you love me?

Christy Yes.

Carmel More than your pigeons?

Christy Lots more.

Carmel Even if they have whiter breasts.

Christy They don't.

Carmel Maybe it's time you checked for yourself? (*They embrace*) Things will work out, Christy. Anyone can lose their job, even Richard Nixon.

Christy I'm better looking than him. More like Johnny Weissmuller they used to say.

They kiss, stage right, as **Dessie** *enters from the left, doing stretching exercises.*

Dessie I never joined a running club. The only person I ran against was myself. That summer when Da lost his job Liverpool beat Newcastle in the Cup Final and a clatter of girls got crushed at some David Cassidy concert in London. I only knew one girl who hadn't a crush on him.

Marie enters and stands beside him as they mime jogging on the spot, while, on the far side of the stage, Christy silently exits.

Marie   Told you I was faster.

Dessie   Where did you come from?

Marie   Think you own the St Margaret's Road?

Dessie   Be careful passing the caravans. Sometimes the kids throw rocks.

Marie   How far do you go?

Dessie   To Pass if You Can.

Marie   What' that?

Dessie   The name of a crossroads, near Dunsogley castle.

Marie   That's miles away.

Dessie   Go home so.

Marie You pass if you can.

They exit in different directions, leaving **Carmel** *alone on stage.*

Carmel Christy wasn't the only one who couldn't say what they felt. The high-rise blues. For years after losing the baby I'd dream about suckling her at my breast and then wake to find nothing except empty space in my arms. Christy snoring away and me listening to the clank of the lift shaft. At every hour of the night somebody coming or going, with the heat of those radiators suffocating the room. Whenever I woke from that dream I'd go out onto the balcony where Christy's pigeons were. Maybe it was being so high up ... the maze of distant lights ... but I felt isolated and tired. After seven years I was tired of waiting for Ballymun to be finished. You saw it in the other mothers too, a different tiredness than our mas had known. (**Jane** *enters from the left.*) The tiredness of climbing stairs when the lifts were broken. The tiredness of waiting for shops to be built, then being unable to afford anything in them with Christy so long out of work. The tiredness of waiting for buses that rarely came. The tiredness of dealing with a Corporation who forbid Christy to hammer a nail into their precious walls, yet never sent anyone to fix anything broken.

Jane and **Carmel** (*standing side by side now*) The tiredness of searching for another ten-penny piece to put into the slot in the hired television.

Carmel The tiredness each night when you realised that you faced the exact same struggle tomorrow and every tomorrow to come.

Jane The tiredness of lying awake in a bed that used to hold two. The tiredness of being unable to sleep with the noise of squatters overhead. (**Carmel** *exits as* **Jane** *moves downstage and* **Marie** *enters to stand behind her.*) After Derek left I knew I could not afford to stay in Pinewood Crescent, but I never thought I'd wind up here. I wanted to leave Pinewood before the man from the building society came to repossess the house, but the social worker's advice was clear – stay to be evicted and the Corporation will have to house you.

Marie *enters softly behind her.*

Marie It's two a.m., Mam, what are you doing sitting up?

Jane Just waiting for them upstairs to finish their party.

Marie That party hasn't finished for the past two years. You have to try and sleep.

Jane The tablets don't work any more, they make my head fuzzy, I was never fuzzy. I keep thinking I'll wake up and be anywhere but Ballymun.

Marie Ballymun is okay, Ma, you just have to get used to it.

Jane I refuse to get used to it. I hate having people look at my girls and thinking …

Marie Thinking what?

Jane God forgive me. There's nothing more pathetic than a snob with no arse in her trousers. I remember watching these towers go up from the bedroom window in Pinewood and wondering how anyone could live here. Your daddy organised a plebiscite to change the postal address of the area to Glasnevin and build a wall to keep us safe from this sort.

Carmel *enters stage right, with* **Jane** *turning to watch her.*

Carmel It was lonely when so many of the original tenants left, families like us who'd came here agog by the newness of everything. I missed their innocence. The newer tenants had a different attitude. We were sent here as a reward, but they saw it as a sentence. Suddenly Ballymun had become a holding camp for awkward cases. The other flats on this floor kept changing hands. The Brennans left first, then the McGraths and Kellys. They had a few bob, their men still in work. The atmosphere changed. Some new neighbours would live in your ear and makes candles from the wax. Others made it plain you should mind your own business. One family piled all their possessions in the lift in one go. Six hours they were stuck, with children screaming. Afterwards, even when the lifts worked, they wouldn't use them. I was scared of the lifts myself but it wasn't wise to show fear. You learnt to walk a certain way. Not that you were scared of your neighbours but as the 1970s wore on you didn't know who your neighbours were any more.

Carmel *exits as* **Marie** *moves downstage, past* **Jane**.

Marie Every evening my ma washed floors in an office block in town. The other cleaners teased her for wearing rubber gloves. Not in a hurtful way, because they saw she was fragile. In the holidays I wanted to work with her but she wouldn't allow that. She could tolerate it herself, but her daughter wasn't going to do it. That was the problem. I lived in Ballymun, yet she wouldn't let me be part of it. Every Saturday we were dressed in our best clothes and brought to view houses for sale in Drumcondra and Glasnevin. Maybe with the Valium Mam half believed that one day we might afford one. It was her fantasy world, examining gardens and converted kitchens. She always gave our old address in Pinewood Crescent to the estate agent.

Jane So what if I did? Could I not cling to one fragment of respectability? If I said I was from these towers the estate agents would have followed me around, thinking I might pinch something. It was my harmless fantasy. At night when the squatters got too loud I would imagine us living in some house I had viewed, arranging flowers in the window and opening the back door to stand with dew-drenched grass under my bare soles.

Marie (*turns to* **Jane**, *urgent whisper*) Mam! Mam!

Jane What?

Marie The Quinns from Pinewood Villas are after coming in behind us. I saw Mrs Quinn staring at the address we gave the estate agent.

Jane I don't want to meet her.

Marie You've as much right to look at this house as that interfering old bag.

Jane Don't call her that.

Marie It's the truth.

Jane She'll tell the whole of Pinewood about me pretending to afford a house when I can barely afford food for us. Is there a side entrance we can slip out?

Marie I'm sick of looking at houses, Mammy, and so is Sharon. We'll walk out that front door. (*Moves away from*

Jane *to stand alone, facing the audience.*) The estate agent was waiting. Just to reconfirm our address. I told him he had it right, but to keep an eye out. There was a Mrs Quinn upstairs, a lying kleptomaniac from Finglas always up before the courts for pinching things.

Jane That was the night when I realised that nine-year-old Sharon stole things. A tiny plastic dog that came in a box of Cornflakes. It had been in a child's room in the house we looked at. Sharon had it pressed in her fist as she slept, like she needed something to cling on to. I knew it was my fault, my unease she was growing up with. Gently I prized it from her as she slept. I went out to the balcony and let it fall, knowing it would break into pieces like everything else here. I never brought my children to look at houses again. But it was too late. Something had started inside my little girl that I had no idea how to deal with.

Jane *moves to stand in isolation at the back of the stage as* **Dessie** *enters to stand beside* **Marie**.

Dessie Marie and me didn't hang out much together in Ballymun because we would have been slagged. Not that girls weren't always getting off with blokes, or so it seemed from how boys bragged about a feel of this or that, their tongue down someone's mouth in a tower-block basement. All made up, I suppose. Her classmates were worse, Marie said, nothing in trousers was safe. We didn't discuss sex when we ran together, we just thought about it. (*They both begin to mime running*) Her white shorts like hot pants and her legs that carried on forever. Pass if You Can became 'make a pass if you can' and I didn't know how to. We discussed the old countrymen watching from cottages in Dubber and the ruins of a Norman keep we explored in a field of wheat early one summer's morning. Just us two alone and how I longed to kiss and touch her ... God, I was the world's biggest coward. We ran back to Ballymun afterwards, not a word between us, like we were angry with each other or both angry with me.

They both exit, passing **Jane**.

Jane Marie was seeing some fellow and, God forgive me, but I didn't like it because he came from the towers. I wanted her having no attachments that would make it hard to leave if the chance came. I'd never met the boy but often saw his father wandering around with one arm longer than the other, waiting for dole day like the other dossers. To be fair, he did nixers and favours, but I had a suspicion of men who were good with their hands and obliging to neighbours. Still, he helped me the first time Sharon went missing. I couldn't keep her indoors all day. I let her down to play on the grass where I could see her. One minute she was there, the next she'd disappeared, and I ran down to shout at the hatchet-faced girls sitting on the wall who simply shrugged. It was my

comeuppance for being considered snooty, no one
bothering to help until he came along.

Christy (*rises from his seat*)   Don't panic, Missus, we'll
find her.

Jane   Don't panic. Even in my state I wished to God that
I wasn't wearing that ancient blue dress. (**Christy** *steps up
onto the stage.*) He got some of the lazy bitches on the
wall to search Balcurris and told others to see had she
crossed the motorway towards Coultry. It was he who
spotted her leaning over the balcony of where the
squatters lived. We both just ran and thank God the lift
was working and the squatters' flat wide open with music
blaring and people sprawled about. (**Jane** *moves forward
with* **Christy** *behind her.*) This was the first time I ever
saw drugs. Zombies with skeletal faces shrugging when I
screamed for Sharon. It was him who picked her up
gently as she leaned right over the railings to stare down.
A young man kept laughing and talking rubbish to her
and Christy – that's what he said his name was – cradled
my ten-year-old like she was a precious object he'd lost.
(**Christy** *has cupped his hands over as if cradling an
imaginary bird or a child.*) And I wasn't afraid of the
squatters, because his eyes made it clear that he would kill
the first one to block our path or touch her.

Christy *turns from* **Jane** (*who exits*) *and confronts* **Dessie**
who enters from the left. **Christy**'*s hands remain cupped.*

Dessie (*alarmed*)   What are you doing with the pigeons, Da?

Christy   I'm breaking up the loft, giving the stupid bastards away. You're not allowed feed them if they fly back to this kip.

Dessie   But you love your pigeons, Da.

Christy   Little gurriers around here have already wrung half their necks. Do you want me to let the rest be killed the same way? They're meant to be homing pigeons; their instincts should tell them this is no bloody home.

Dessie   It is home.

Christy   Not for me.

Dessie   Well it is for me and you can't take that away. I don't remember Bolton Street. I love this flat and hate you always going on about Ballymun. I belong here even if you don't.

Christy   This isn't how Ballymun was meant to be.

Dessie   But it's the way it is.

Christy   I was somebody in Bolton Street. Neighbours came to me to write letters for them. Here I'm nobody, not even a proper father.

Dessie Stop fighting with Ma and you might feel like one. Real fathers do more than shout.

Christy Real fathers go to work and people look at them instead of looking through them.

Dessie You'll get a job again.

Christy Who are you codding? (*Looks down*) Do you want this last pigeon?

Dessie The pigeons are yours. I'm no good with them.

Christy (*turning his back and letting his hands fall*) Fine so.

Dessie You bastard. You killed it.

Christy (*exiting*) I wish someone would do the same for me.

Dessie *turns to* **Carmel** *who enters.*

Carmel He's jarred, son. We had a visitation from the dole office. You'd swear we were sheltering Lord Lucan from how they swarmed in. A tip off about your da doing a nixer last week. He didn't even get paid for it. With the lousy few bob they give us to live on he has to be doing something. Otherwise he'll go mad and by Christ he'll drive me daft too.

Marie (*entering*)   The seventies were tough, the news always about oil prices and stock markets collapsing. It was like the Wall Street crash, only if the bosses whose offices my ma cleaned wanted to jump properly to their deaths the only buildings in Dublin high enough were in Ballymun, and there was no fear of them traipsing out here. What I hated most was the music – Telly Savalas or that awful *Honey I Miss You* being played at the discos. I liked *Tiger Feet*.

She begins to sing the song with **Dessie** *and* **Carmel** *joining in, dancing with* **Marie** *as* **Carmel** *exits and* **Dessie** *goes into an air-guitar solo that makes him sink to his knees and then simply lie on his back.*

Marie (*sitting beside him*)   Dessie had the neatest bum running on his tiger feet. If he'd kissed me I couldn't have talked to him. But he seemed more like a brother and didn't mind what I said, even when I put my foot in it about his da, because a darkness hung over his da back then. You needed to be careful here with young fellows prowling around, wolf-whistling, as I was always trying to tell Sharon. But older blokes like Dessie's da were scarier. They didn't hassle you but there was something dead in their eyes. You saw them waiting for the pub to open, going in to nurse pints that turned mouldy, watch horse racing or – some people said – blue movies. Coming out half cocked in every sense. Dessie never liked discussing him. (*She playfully straddles* **Dessie**) Open wider, I told

Dessie one day, lying on the grass by the holy well at St Margaret's. Open wider, and me laughing, trying to cram grass into his mouth, practising to be a dental assistant. Dessie tried to close his mouth but I held his jaw tight, and – gobshite that I was – didn't I go and kiss him because he was almost fifteen and it was about time somebody did. (*They kiss. She lifts her head as his hands flail about*) And I felt an electric shock through his body and through mine. And didn't I wear the mouth off him with his hands all over me like a blind man on a train seeking the emergency cord. Only his hands were not allowed inside my clothes, thank you (*she slaps his hand*), and my hands planned no excursions down under, at least not until I got a visa for Australia. (*She rises and* **Dessie** *rises also, walking as if in a dream to the back of the stage.*) At the end we were hot and bothered and frustrated and running back to Ballymun, silently panting, and I knew that was the last bit of decent conversation I'd get out of him for ages to come.

Marie *exits and* **Dessie** *turns, love-struck.*

Dessie   I couldn't stop thinking of her. Pacing my room at night, looking across at her tower block, imagining Marie asleep wearing God knows what or nothing at all. I loved living up here at this green height, the air pure when I opened my window, the world distant. (**Christy** *enters and goes to front of stage, left.*) Often there was the sound of Ma and Da arguing or not talking at all. But I didn't really take that in any more because I was in love and pacing about up here where nothing could touch me.

Dessie *sits at the back of the stage, facing away from the audience as* **Carmel** *enters and approaches* **Christy.**

Carmel   Are you going to sit out on this balcony all night? Come to bed for God's sake.

Christy   Why? I'd only have to get up again.

Carmel   You could try keeping me warm. Or have you forgotten how to do that too?

Christy   I'll come in in a while.

Carmel   Of course you can't have forgotten. Not with the films I hear that some hardchaws show in their flats after closing time. A gaggle of drunk men peering at strangers having sex.

Christy   I don't watch those films.

Carmel   I think you do and it scares me because I can't compete with some twenty-year-old porn star. Maybe I haven't the breasts I once had, but am I really so old and haggard? Can you not even bear to be in the same bed?

Christy   What do you want off me? I'm not a teenager with a permanent erection on demand.

Carmel   I want hope. I want to be made feel special.

Christy Maybe I can't do that any more. You can only feel special when you think you're going somewhere. We've reached the terminus. Our lives have stopped.

Carmel Maybe we need to get out and push.

Christy I'm too exhausted.

Carmel What gives you the right to be exhausted? Do you think you're the only unemployed man in Dublin? Is hammering nails so bloody important for you?

Christy Supporting my family is.

Carmel There's more than one kind of support, Christy, and these last years you've been a dead weight around my neck. I drag shopping up those stairs, I drag myself but I don't see why I should have to drag you. I'm off to bed. (**Carmel** *goes to exit, then stops and looks back*) Take a good look at the view and if all you're good for is looking, then go back to the porn films or give us all a break and fucking jump.

She exits as **Christy** *turns to the audience.*

Christy I knew she was awake, lying in bed by the window. I stood right up on the balcony. I'd never leaned so far over. I had to close my eyes to stop myself swaying. Even with them shut I knew every light in every tower block and the city beyond. All the roads leading to other places. This was the view my slaughtered pigeons had memorised, somehow always finding their way back. My arms were outstretched, moving slightly, the way I'd seen them mark time in the air. Their ghosts were around me. I could feel their forgiveness and silent companionship and knew that if I leaned forward they would not break my fall. They would glide alongside me as I tumbled through the air and for those few seconds I could pretend to belong with them, like I pretended to belong among the hard men in the pub. I felt a sudden sense of power because for once I had a choice. I could step back and live or lean forward and die. I knew that Carmel didn't want me to make this choice for her or Dessie. She wanted me to make it for myself alone, my decision to live or die. I wasn't sure how far I was over the balcony and if I opened my eyes the fright alone might make me fall. So I stepped back with the slowest, most deliberate step I ever made and held my hands outstretched, with my palms aloft for the pigeons to perch there. Of course the pigeons were dead and I was alone and exhausted. But a woman awaited me in bed and I was coming back to her, like a hunter after a long journey. And I knew and she knew – even if no one else could see it and people looked down on my poverty – that I was not returning empty-handed.

Dessie (*turns to face the audience and rises*)   I don't know what woke me – not a noise, more a foreboding like the world stood balanced on one moment. (**Christy**, *alone at the front of the stage, raises his arms out in a slow, Christ-like gesture as* **Carmel** *enters from the right.*) From my window I saw Da lean across the railing, hands outstretched, and I knew his eyes were closed and if I called out he would topple forward. In that moment it felt like I didn't know this stranger. It was the stupidest feeling but I was half convinced he could fly; I kept waiting for him to glide. I was scared for him and for myself and I wanted to pray. But I could do nothing except watch until he stepped back and walked slowly indoors and I knew that I could never ask him about this moment.

Christy *lowers his arms and turns to approach* **Carmel** *with* **Dessie** *walking downstage to stand near them, a family again.*

Carmel That was the night Christy came to me shaking with desire, the night I stayed his hand reaching for the condoms in the bedside drawer. The night we threw caution to the wind and afterwards lay in each other's arms, instinctively knowing that a child was conceived. The night we started to live again, when, for better or worse, in sickness or health, we staked our claim here to the future.

Lights down. End of Act One.

ACT TWO

Lights come up on characters arrayed on stage. **Dessie** *and* **Marie** *sit together, with* **Tara** *behind them, and the others stand nearby.*

Dessie It was 1977.

Christy The Sex Pistols were being unleashed from their holsters, God help us. Dessie was studying hard up in the Comprehensive and I'd become a worker again.

Carmel I'd become a mother again.

Jane (*Relieved*) I hadn't become a granny yet, thank God, though I was always warning Marie about lads from the flats.

Dessie I'd become a semi-official punk rocker ... at least when Ma wasn't watching.

Carmel (*distracted aside*) Where in God's name are all the safety pins going?

Marie My kid sister gave up being a Bay City Rollers fan ... Sharon said they were a bit too young for her.

Tara And my parents split up.

The others look at her, slightly shocked.

Marie 'Split up' is a bit extreme.

Dessie We hadn't properly got together yet.

Marie If left to Dessie we probably never would have. (*Turns to him, exasperated*) For God's sake, would you just kiss me!

Marie *briefly kisses* **Dessie** *as* **Tara** *exits in embarrassed disgust and* **Christy** *steps forward to stand beside* **Carmel.** *and the* **Junkie** *exit to their seats, while* **Sharon** *goes to sit quietly near the front of the stage and* **Dessie** *and* **Marie** *remain seated on stage, intently watching* **Christy** *and* **Carmel.**

Christy We both knew the risk in conceiving that child. Carmel was afraid to visit her own doctor after him warning her. Me pacing outside petrified, when she was getting the result.

Carmel I simply needed a child to start again. A friend in Pearse Tower said I was mad to risk it at my age. She mentioned English clinics where such things could be sorted out safely, not like the old quack nurses in Dublin bedsits. She made me feel a hundred and six. I was only forty-two. My Ma had the last of us at forty-six and was up getting the dinner two days later. I didn't judge the girls who slipped off to England, but sure I wouldn't have known how to get there anyway and having to try and fill in the forms would have made me look stupid. No, this baby was meant to kill or cure us, because carrying him made me feel good about myself for the first time in years.

Christy The job centre would send me for interviews and it was mainly a load of bollix, to keep themselves employed shuffling papers. But my luck turned at the Wire and Cable factory in Finglas. It was basic work, hammering slats to seal the spools of roadside electric cable, but it felt good to hammer a nail again. I started three weeks before the child was born. Another son … the instructions for girls must have been in Japanese. When he was born I finally felt that I belonged out here. Waking to his cries … walking to work at seven in the morning, wrecked but nicely wrecked with good cause.

Dessie (*rises to face* **Christy** *as* **Marie** *exits*) Visiting Ma in hospital I felt more like an uncle than a brother. Da and me had our first pint together opposite the Rotunda, in a corner where the barman couldn't spot how I was a year away from shaving.

Carmel (*sits at the front of the stage*) And I lived through the birth and the baby lived too, despite the anxious faces and being brought in early and kept on drips and young Charlie – as we called him …

Christy (*proudly, as he exits*) After Charles J. Haughey, my hero, whose star was rising again.

Carmel … being kept in an incubator. And when we brought him home by bus half of Ballymun called into our flat, sharing our happiness, and I felt part of something, like young Charlie had become a link between neighbours with nothing else in common.

Jane *has risen to approach* **Carmel**.

Jane (*Awkwardly*) I was just passing … I'm Marie's mum … your Desmond pals around with her … that's all they do, I hope … (*Looks down at* **Carmel***'s arms*) Isn't the baby beautiful?

Jane *passes by and sits on the stage, looking away.*

Carmel Lady Muck wouldn't be in it. 'Your Desmond.' Made him sound like a stable boy. Still, she wasn't a bad sort, just a bit lost, like she could only cling on to some notion of respectability by looking down on everyone else. I wouldn't mind, but it was known that she had her own problems with her youngest.

Marie *enters to urgently tug at* **Dessie***'s hand.*

Marie Will you help me look for Sharon?

Dessie Where could she be this time?

Marie She's mad enough to be anywhere. Fourteen and acting like she's thirty-four. Boys bore her, she said last night, she preferred men with lived-in eyes. I promised my mam to look after Sharon while she's in work, but short of using handcuffs I don't know how.

Sharon *rises at the front of the stage to confront them.*

Dessie We found her sitting in a stairwell in Shangan, smoking, a slight tremble in her hand. The back of her T- shirt was black from the wall where gurriers had lit a fire.

Sharon He said I reminded him of Olga Korbut. I'd know him to see again – he had teeth like an American.

Marie You stupid little bitch, have you no sense? What did you let him do to you?

Sharon What's it to you? At least one of us knows how to have a good time. Your biggest dream is to help people spit into paper cups at the dentist.

Sharon *and* **Dessie** *exit, leaving* **Marie** *looking at* **Jane** *sitting alone who rises.*

Jane Something happened to my baby that I couldn't understand. There was a void in her that nothing could fill. The most affectionate child, needing to be cuddled, acting out innocent fantasies with her teddies. Then one day the fantasies took over and a stranger stared from my daughter's eyes. The queue in the health centre, a doctor firing questions – had she hallucinations, mood-swings, missed her father. Could she simply be growing up?

Marie Mum, the principal called me out of class again today, asking where Sharon was. I wouldn't mind only I left her walking down the corridor towards her classroom.

Jane (*turns to* **Marie**) Did you not check that she went in?

Marie I'm studying for the Leaving, trying to keep up.

Jane (*sharply*) I told you to mind her in school.

Marie And at night when you're in work.

Jane You think I like cleaning offices? Do you not think there are days when I feel like jumping from this balcony?

Marie Don't say that.

Jane I wouldn't do it because I have you and your sister to mind. That's what keeps me going and I need your help.

Marie I feel like shaking the little cow. Where is she now?

Jane In the bedroom doing homework.

Marie I've just come from the bedroom.

Jane   Good Jesus, she hasn't gone again.

Jane *exits as* **Marie** *looks across the stage to the seats on the right where* **Christy** *rises.*

Christy (*calls*)   Dessie, a lady caller. (*To* **Marie**, *closer look, concerned*) Are you all right?

Marie   Sharon's gone missing again.

Dessie (*entering from left*)   I won't be long, Ma, I'll study when I come in.

Marie   We were always long, searching for hours then giving up. Those searches became our dates.

Dessie *stands close to her, and they kiss passionately, then* **Marie** *breaks away.*

Marie   That's far enough for tonight.

Dessie   You let me go further on the last bus.

Marie   The back of the bus is safer than the back of Pappin's Church. I don't want us going too far. (*They kiss again, passionately, then* **Marie** *surfaces for air*) Not that I don't want to, but I can't. (*Beat*) Eileen Ferguson is pregnant.

Dessie (*shocked*)   But she's only sixteen …

Marie   She'll sit the Leaving but she and Steve are getting married straight after. They hope to live with her folks, only she hasn't told them yet. Steve gave her a ring to wear outside the house, but I bet he runs away to England.

Dessie   You know I'd never do that, don't you?

Marie   So how come you sit bolt upright like a startled rabbit whenever they show ads in the Savoy cinema for the Happy Ring House Jewellers.

Dessie   I do not.

Marie   All boys do. There are hands popping out of blouses in the back row like they got an electric shock.

Dessie   I love you.

Marie   I can't hear you.

Dessie   I said, I love you.

Marie   I can't afford to hear you, Dessie. You're going nowhere.

Dessie   I work hard at school.

Marie   For what? There's no opportunity here. You'll

find a dead-end job and the worst thing is that you'll be happy in it.

Dessie   Is being happy a sin?

Marie   It's a trap. After the Leaving Cert I'm getting a few bob together and a working holiday visa to Australia and I'll find some way to stay out there.

Dessie   What about Sharon and your mother?

Marie   I've been carrying my mother's pain on my back since I was ten, listening to her cry with loneliness at night. What do you want me to do, Dessie, sink under that weight?

Dessie   What about me?

Marie   Pack your bag and come away too, somewhere where they've never heard of Ballymun. (*No reply.*) You say 'Ma, Da, I'm leaving,' then pack your bag and we go.

Dessie   To do what?

Marie   Live.

Dessie   I live here.

Christy and **Carmel** *quietly enter on opposite side of stage.*

Marie You exist.

Dessie Waking up somewhere else won't change who I am.

Marie But I don't want to wake up here any more, Dessie. That's a pity because it means I'll never wake up beside you.

Marie *exits, hurt, as* **Dessie** *sits on the stage, away from his parents.*

Carmel Charlie loved the story of being wheeled down in his pram to join the blockade when builders tried to bulldoze the site for the swimming pool. In his mind it was he who forced them to finally build that pool. He acted like he owned it, a water baby with inflated armbands. By his fourth birthday I was the one in armbands trying to keep up. When I was a kid us girls went down the canal mainly to see boys in their knicks diving in. I was always scared of the old prams buried among the weeds where your feet might get stuck. I never learnt to swim because I'd no need to. It was like writing. I did it in school but spent my days dying to turn fourteen so I could earn money. Everything was taught through Irish, which I didn't understand, and the real lesson you learnt was never to draw attention to yourself. That way you'd less chance of getting belted. When I started in the tinned-meat factory in Marrowbone Lane you didn't need writing, you needed a strong stomach.

The same when I got a better job in the sewing factory where girls sang all day. And didn't I marry an educated man who signed any forms that needed signing. It became our little secret and I'd no cause to read anything in Ballymun where the only sign ever put up was 'Out of Order'. I could shop by knowing things by sight, memorising the labels from ads on the telly. God knows I'd have loved to help Dessie with his studies, but Dessie was bright as a button and knew to ask his da. But Charlie was my precious gift and I longed to do things with him like other mas. The Ladybird books were great in the new library because they had a tape so I could learn the words by heart and pretend to read them aloud, hugging him on my knee and yet ashamed at deceiving my own son.

Christy   I was working the night shift that week. I loved the sound of six-inch nails slotting into wood. Sitting around at three in the morning, eating ham sambos and swapping yarns. The world asleep except us. Then dawn over the skylights and the last hours flew. (*He crosses the stage, passing* **Dessie**) We'd walk home together, men peeling off at every corner. At that hour Ballymun always looked different, deserted. A few horses tied up on the grass. Maybe a stolen car tipped onto its side. Carmel would have a blanket over the bedroom curtains and I always felt I wouldn't sleep, yet I did. That Tuesday I woke to the sound of Dessie coming in (**Dessie** *rises, looks at* **Carmel** *and then at* **Christy**'s *back*) and knew he was outside the bedroom door, dying to talk, yet not wanting to disturb me. (*Turns*) Come in, will you.

Dessie (*slightly stunned*) Da, I got the Leaving Cert.

Christy You passed it.

Dessie I got four honours.

Christy Four honours. Holy shite. (*To* **Carmel**) Do you hear that, Carmel? Four honours. Nobody in our family ever even did the Leaving before. The boy's a genius. Four honours would get you into university, wouldn't it?

Dessie We don't have the money, Da.

Christy We can find the money.

Dessie We can't. I'll get a job, study at night.

Christy Well, we can find the money for a bloody drink, you and me. Four honours, I always said that with my looks and your mother's brains you'd go far. (**Carmel** *exits, upset*) What did I say?

Dessie Forget it, Da.

Christy You're all getting so sensitive you'll be hugging trees next.

Christy *puts his arm around* **Dessie** *and they stagger across the stage, singing an Elvis song.*

Dessie That afternoon was the first time I ever got drunk with my da. Staggering home together, we met Marie.

They stop singing and observe her.

Christy (*drunk*) A 'B' in Geography. Well, he grew up with homing pigeons. Best sense of geography in the world, pigeons, little soft breasts … (*Stops, looks at* **Marie**) I'd better go to work, son, if they don't sack me.

He exits off, singing.

Dessie How were your results?

Marie Good. All the girls from the Comprehensive are going into Zhivago's nightclub.

Dessie Are you going with them?

Marie To be groped for a clatter of Southsiders? What will you do?

Dessie Get drunk, I suppose … well, drunker …

Marie Run it off.

Dessie   I can barely walk.

Marie   Well, you'll never catch me, so.

Dessie   Wait for me.

Marie   I told you years ago. A girl with her skirt up runs faster.

They begin to circle each other on the stage, drawing ever closer.

Dessie   We ran through the August evening, past the Travellers' encampment, past ruined fields where cider drinkers slumped at bonfires, past bricked-up cottages with Marie leading the way.

Marie   Looking back and laughing and knowing I'd never forget this moment. When I turned into old Silloge Lane he caught up and we kissed (*they kiss*), panting, before I broke free ...

Dessie   Her tight white jeans and body arching as she ran ...

Marie   His stupid bloody army jacket and long hair and elephant flares ...

Dessie   And when she stopped near the stream ...

In each other's arms now, they slide to the ground, with **Dessie** *on top, kissing passionately.*

Marie   I knew that he knew how much I wanted the feel of him inside me …

Dessie (*looks up to address audience*)   I'd been carrying around that bloody condom I bought from a school pal for so long that I was afraid it would be mouldy.

They kiss a last time, then the embrace dissolves and they lie slightly apart, staring up.

Marie   And we lay in the dark for a long time after just looking up.

Dessie   I can't believe the stars are so bright.

Marie   The further you go from Ballymun the brighter they get.

Dessie (*sits up to look at her*)   Don't ruin it.

Marie   Nothing could ruin tonight. I could dance.

Dessie   Say you love me.

Marie   I've shown it.

Dessie   That's not the same.

Marie (*slightly annoyed*)   You've done well. Don't complain.

He rises and she sits up, cross-legged, shoulders slightly hunched up.

Dessie   We walked home, the towers rising up, bonfires blazing in fields, gougers out of their skulls with cider and dope. Heat still pulsing through my body, but I felt cold too, like I'd been tricked. I had longed so much for Marie, yet I knew that I was losing her, this was her parting gift.

He lifts up the suitcase, which has been resting unseen behind the ramp, and places it down beside **Marie** *who does not look up.* **Jane** *enters from the opposite side of the stage.*

Jane   The Corporation evicted the squatters upstairs, but another crowd simply moved in and stayed until one of their parties ended with a faller from the balcony. No one knew his name. The Corporation boarded up that flat and two plain-clothes Jesuits moved into the flat below me. Nice, courageous men, the most robbed priests in Ireland. Other tenants kept coming and going, their problems dumped on us. When a deputation ordered me to stop paying rent till the lifts were properly fixed, I told them I'd always paid my way and to mind their own business. After that most tenants ostracised me. I'd never felt more alone, with Marie working in an office by day and in McDonald's at night, desperate to save up and escape, leaving me alone with Sharon whom I couldn't properly talk to any more.

Carmel (*from her seat*) I saw a change in Dessie after he finished school. It took him six months to find work. I kept saying to use his uncle's address in Broadstone: they see Ballymun on an application form and tear it up. But Dessie was pig-headed like his da, the pair of them arguing of an evening.

Dessie It wasn't the lack of work that got to me. It was Marie avoiding me. Saw her in Sloopy's nightclub French kissing some Neolithic waster who'd lumbered down from his cave in Cabra to leave fingerprints all over her arse. I got wasted that night, walking home past Hampstead Park, with couples pressed against the hedgerows. Finally got a job in the end as a storeman in a warehouse. I started a night course in Kevin Street Tech and tried to forget Marie because she seemed to want to forget me.

Dessie *sits at the back of the stage, facing away from the audience, as* **Jane** *goes to sit beside* **Marie**. *They are awkward with each other.*

Jane Are you packed?

Marie I've probably bought too much, but I don't know when I'll be back. They say that when the visa runs out you can find work on the black once you don't try to leave the country. Dessie is arranging a lift. I called in to say goodbye to his folks. His little brother Charlie is a howl.

Jane You'll miss him.

Marie He could have come. (*Beat*) Mam, you know this is what I always wanted.

Jane (*rises*) Am I stopping you? I'm just annoyed that Sharon isn't here to say good-bye. One of many broken promises. She was happy in Pinewood before I brought her here.

Marie (*rises also*) She was a child. All children are happy. Junkies come from private houses too.

Jane (*raises a hand as if to slap her*) Don't call your sister that.

Marie (*shocked*) You never hit me in your life.

Jane (*lowers her hand wearily*) Maybe I should have. Maybe I should have let neither of you out the door of this flat. What sort of mother have I been?

Marie The best you could be. We're tearing each other apart as usual, with Sharon away getting stoned.

Jane She knows you're leaving for Australia. Wait twenty minutes and she'll be here.

Marie Wait another twenty and she'll have rifled every penny I've saved to get there.

Jane Your sister is no thief.

Marie Mam, why are you lying? You know nothing is safe with her, in a purse, a chemist shop or in trousers. I love her and I hate what she is doing to you but she'll end up in prison or dead and you know it. (*Sits, weary*) I can't go and leave you alone like this. You're more important to me.

Jane (*kneels to take **Marie**'s hand in hers*) Then for my sake go before you get tied down here. One minute I was a carefree girl dancing at Red Island. The next minute I had you in my womb. '*I'll only put it in a little bit*,' the first of your father's many promises. You felt like a ball and chain. Your father doing his duty, choosing confetti over shotgun pellets. I grew to love you but you curtailed my dreams. I know you love me, but if you stay for my sake you'll resent me and I'd sooner be lonely than have that.

Marie (*tenderly*) Ma …

Jane (*firmly*) Go.

They embrace as **Dessie** *rises to stand beside the suitcase which he picks up.*

Dessie Marie didn't ask me to go with her, just like I didn't ask her to stay. But we still made love for a last – or, to be precise, second – time. In an actual bed when my folks brought Charlie swimming. She might find other men in Australia, but I knew nobody would ever be this close to her. My mate Tomo, who was a pirate DJ, had a Triumph Herald. You could take the roof down, just never get the bloody thing back up. He drove us to the airport, along the back roads we used to run. My arm around Marie.

Dessie *crosses the stage to place the suitcase down beside* **Marie** *who embraces him.* **Jane** *has stepped to the back of the stage where she stands alone.*

Marie Do me a favour, Dessie. Keep an eye out for Sharon.

Dessie I'll do my best.

Marie You're a good man.

Dessie I'll miss you.

Marie Australian fellows will be rich and better looking and wash their hair more often that you do and I must be an awful gobshite because I'll miss you. Every day I'll miss your stupid grin and your bullshit.

Dessie   You'll miss nothing. When that plane takes off you'll know what it means to be free.

They kiss a last time, then **Marie** *breaks free and* **Dessie** *exits.*

Marie   The plane wheeled in an arc across North Dublin. There, at the weirdest angle below, were the seven towers with smaller blocks arranged around them and all the open spaces. I could name every place and knew that Sharon was down there and my mam and Dessie. And the plane seemed to linger in slow motion over the towers, reluctant to let go. I sat back and knew I wasn't leaving, I would take them with me in my soul wherever I'd go.

Marie *exits and* **Jane** *steps forward.*

Jane   I was truly alone now, arguing with social workers, the guards whenever Sharon was in trouble. It scared me how quickly she moved from coming home reeking of cider, to coming home with pockmarked veins, to not coming home at all. It was like she reached the cliff-edge of childhood and saw nothing beyond it but a vast emptiness. Disaffected was the social worker's term. Ballymun was the place for disaffection, with junkies and dealers playing hide and seek in a warren of boarded-up flats. The two Jesuits urged me to think of myself, do a literacy-tutoring course, spend a few hours a week being someone other than Sharon's mam.

She turns, confronted by **Carmel** *who has entered but now backs away.*

Carmel   Oh, Jesus, not you. No thank you, missus.

Jane   I didn't know you would be my first pupil. They just gave me a Christian name.

Carmel   I came to this prefab to learn to read. It wasn't easy. Shaking out there, lighting cigarette after cigarette. I didn't come to be looked down on.

Jane   What have I to look down on?

Carmel   That never stopped you before.

Jane   Ask them to find you a different tutor.

Carmel   I will. (*Beat*) Nothing personal, but I just don't want anyone to know. I'll not be laughed at.

Jane   Who would I tell in the flats? Do you not think they'd laugh at me, setting myself up as a teacher when I clean offices at night?

Carmel You'd make a good teacher. For someone else. Do you miss your daughter in Australia? She writes to Dessie.

Jane What does she say? (*Realisation*) Christ, that was stupid …

Carmel I couldn't be your spy, even if I wanted to. If you see Dessie … don't tell him I came here.

Jane They'll find you another tutor.

Carmel I'll see. I've come this far without reading and I'm no one's fool. Good luck, missus.

Jane The name is Jane. It either stands for Plain Jane or for Calamity.

Carmel *exits as* **Dessie** *enters.*

Dessie Before Marie went away Jane and me were suspicious of each other. But now I'd occasionally call in, with both of us missing Marie badly. I'd talk about finishing my course in Kevin Street, getting elected shop steward in my new job, girls I was half-heartedly seeing. Jane was a fine-looking woman. I was walking home from a party at dawn one Sunday when I saw her wandering around the flats.

Jane (*approaches* **Dessie,** *desperate*) I haven't seen her for four days. She could be lying in some flat, raped or over-dosed with rat poison. For God's sake, Dessie, help me find her.

Dessie Sharon wasn't hard to find. Part of a lost skeletal congregation jockeying around their priest. A bit-player dealer in Dunne's Stores white socks who looked close to death himself. An old pair of sneakers swung from the ESB cables, but these junkies needed no sign: they could smell the fear that there mightn't be enough heroin to go around. Sharon was being pushed among the scrum of people waving cash, trying to barter whatever they'd stolen the previous night. I felt sick, suddenly convinced there were ghosts around me I couldn't see – children who died of fever, the starving natives from the townlands of Balcurris and Coultry who'd congregated at dawn around a penal mass rock, migrant labourers succumbing to cholera in the ditches. For those seconds I felt sure that Ballymun had a beating soul and the ghosts of its unknown dead were watching.

During this speech **Sharon** *has entered to kneel behind* **Dessie,** *her back to the audience, shivering.*

Jane A cop car crossed the grass and the junkies scattered, fleeing back towards the parts of Dublin they had drifted in from. Sharon put a small plastic bag in her mouth and ran. I tried to follow but she was too fast.

Jane *stands at the back of the stage as* **Dessie** *approaches* **Sharon**.

Dessie   I promised to bring her home. I didn't want Jane entering any shooting gallery. Sharon legged it across the motorway, with all composure gone. She had her gear and now had to have it inside her.

Sharon (*to herself, shaking*)   So hard to find a vein … where have they all gone … (*Looks up, seeing* **Dessie**) What do you want, shithead?

Dessie   To bring you home.

Sharon   You screwed my sister, you probably screwed my mother. You want to make it a hat trick, do you?

Dessie   Take your gear. You can go off as easily at home as here at the back of Pappin's Church. At least you'll be safe.

Sharon   I'll only be safe when this is inside me. You want to help, then light this fucking candle because my hand is shaking.

Dessie   It's filthy here.

Sharon   I can't wait. Help me.

...uctantly he kneels to put an arm around her.

Jane   Squeeze the lemon. I had to haunt pubs for a few bits left in glasses. Bloody barmen chasing you out.

Still kneeling, **Dessie** *looks back at the audience as* **Sharon** *mimes injecting herself.*

Dessie   I did the bare minimum. This wasn't the help Marie had in mind, but Sharon seemed gone to a place where no one could reach her. Every word the slur of a smackhead. Her gizmo was dirty, the sizzle of the gear turning dark on the spoon. She pulled a tourniquet tight with bitter self-hate, begging me to search for a vein. Then, after I don't know how long, I saw blood and knew she'd found one. I turned my back but heard the sigh, like a vampire tasting blood. (**Sharon** *leans back, lolling her head against her arm resting on the side of the stage.*) And when I looked around her face was different. She had the rush with all fear gone and asked me to roll her a joint from some hash in her pocket. I did because if I didn't she would smoke the remaining heroin on some foil and I wanted her to leave that for later so that she wouldn't have to go out robbing. (*He rises and* **Sharon** *rises too.*) She took my hand and walked home to her mother's flat and I felt ... I don't know ... like she was the ghost of my kid sister who'd never properly been born, and I knew she possessed a wondrous light and would never live to see twenty-five.

Dessie *watches* **Sharon** *exit, then follows as* **Carmel** *enters to approach* **Jane.**

Jane   Oh, it's you.

Dessie (*from the side, as if leading a chant*)   What do we want?

Cast (*who begin to line the back of the stage, chanting back once*)   When do we want it?

Carmel   Am I calling at a bad time?

Jane   No, I'm just not used to visitors, unless to do with Sharon. (*Anxious*) She hasn't …?

Carmel   No. She's in jail, isn't she?

Jane   Shoplifting. Even when she's inside I can't stop worrying. You'd think someone would be safe in jail; you'd think they'd get help.

Dessie (*shouts, from the side*)   What do we want?

Cast (*chant*)   When do we want it?

Carmel   I need help. I need you to teach me to read.

Jane   I gave that up. I'm in no position to teach anyone anything. They'll find you another tutor.

Carmel I want someone I can talk to, not an outsider.

Jane I always thought that's what I was.

Carmel You're here so long you're one of us whether you like it or not. I never see you at the protests. Young Charlie loves them. They're closing the bank. Bank of Ireland say they're making no money from people just cashing welfare cheques. With no bank we'll be totally cut off. Tomorrow we plan to block the road, annoy the rich folk who only use Ballymun as a short cut. Come with me. It's a good way to meet folk.

Dessie (*shouts, from the side*) What do we want?

Cast (*chant*) When do we want it?

Jane I meet a lot of people through my daughter.

Carmel Meet other folk trying to change things. If people see us together at the protest they'll think we're friends. They wouldn't think it odd if I call into you. Last week I found a Ladybird book I used to pretend to read to Charlie. These days I say that reading gives me a headache. But I thought I knew the words by heart, 'Mrs Hedgehog is baking a cake ...' He looks up with puzzled eyes. 'Ma, why are you reading the words on the wrong page?' I locked the bathroom door and ran the taps so he couldn't hear me cry at the shame of being caught out by my seven-year-old son.

Dessie (*shouts, from the side*)   What do we want?

Cast (*chant*)   When do we want it?

Jane   Sharon will need all my attention when she gets out. I might be a lousy teacher.

Carmel   Will I see you at the protest?

Jane   Every night when I come home from work men are standing at braziers, armed with sticks, trying to keep out the druggies and dealers. I see them look through me, feel their blame at my failure.

Carmel   It's not blame in their eyes, it's understanding. Do you think they would be out there if they hadn't seen their own children destroyed by junk?

Dessie (*shouts, from the side*)   What do we want?

Cast (*chant*)   When do we want it?

Dessie *and the others (except* **Sharon**) *begin to march in a circle on the stage, making room for* **Jane** *to join them. They repeat their chant.*

Jane (*to audience*)   I joined the protest with Carmel. Naturally the bank didn't listen. They loaded their safe into an armoured car and vanished to richer suburbs. But I found that I liked protesting. I even joined the procession carrying a coffin to the bank headquarters in Baggot Street. And after the bank left, a sense of injustice seemed to rally people. (*She calls out*) What do you want?

They others begin to drift away from her and, whispering 'Drugs Out' with a soft but growing menace, begin to circle **Sharon** *who sits on the opposite side of the stage, scared by their encroachment.*

Jane   There were marches by Concerned Parents Against Drugs, local women offering support, telling stories that matched my own. Sharon came out of jail and tried again to detox, just her and me and her demons going through hell in our flat. After two weeks I felt the worst was over. I relaxed and left the front door ajar for a second. I didn't see her for six days after that.

Jane *crosses the stage to sink down in despair beside* **Sharon** *who is hunched up, shivering. The others have trooped off, no longer whispering.*

Jane   What's happened?

Sharon   Your friends paid us a visit.

Jane   Who?

Sharon   The vigilantes.

Jane   I know them, they wouldn't wreck our flat like this.

Sharon   You don't know them. The paramilitaries have taken control. Half the ringleaders never set foot in Ballymun before. They said I was dealing. I'm not dealing, I was helping a few friends. They said if I wasn't gone within a week they'd throw me off the balcony.

Dessie *and* **Christy** *step forward to help* **Jane** *and* **Sharon** *to rise and comfort them.* **Carmel** *goes to sit at the front of the stage, away from the action.*

Christy   I didn't recognise the ringleaders, but you saw less locals marching, more outsiders urging people to pass information on to them and not the police. Dessie and I slept in Jane's flat for a fortnight, not knowing if it would be attacked or by who. Sharon was rarely there and when she was she seemed like a ghost already.

Jane *drifts to the very back of the stage while* **Sharon** *exits.*

Dessie   Next thing the government introduced a surrender grant for anyone willing to pack up and quit Ballymun. Most of my mates were already long gone. Tomo worked in a nuclear plant in Canada – saved a fortune on electric bills, he glowed in the dark. Johno who sat beside me in school claimed the first graffiti he saw on the Berlin Wall read 'Pearse Tower Rules OK'. I was the one who stayed through thick and thin, maybe because I felt someone had to. Qualifying as an electrician, getting deeper into the trade union movement. But this surrender grant meant that anyone with a few bob would leave, with more flats boarded up or filled by problem tenants or people dumped from mental homes. The day the surrender-grant letter arrived Ma hesitantly began to read it out, getting almost every word right. Me and Da and even little Charlie looking at her like she had started spouting French. (*Approaching* **Carmel** *in bewilderment*) Where did you learn to read, Ma?

Carmel (*rises*) In Ballymun, same as yourself.

Christy (*baffled*) Don't look at me, son.

Carmel So, are we taking this grant or what?

Christy If we have any bloody sense we will. These walls owe us nothing. Two decades of aggravation.

Carmel We're signing so?

Christy (*quickly*) Still we wouldn't want to be hasty. We'll consider our options.

Dessie What does that mean? You always say you hate this place, Da.

Christy I do, son, with an intensity. But there are only two sorts of people. Those who think that Ballymun is brimming with the salt of the earth but would never dream of living here. And then there's those like me who think it's a God-forsaken kip and wouldn't dream of living anywhere else.

Carmel   Mother of God, give me patience.

Christy   I'm just saying that even if the lift stinks and young lads are sleeping rough on the stairs, once we step through our own front door we have the place lovely. It feels like home and Charlie loves it.

Dessie   You'll only be carried out of this flat in a box, Da.

Carmel (*pushing* **Christy** *affectionately off the stage*) Carry? We'll drop him over the balcony for the kids' horses to chew on.

Dessie *sits at the back of the stage as* **Jane** *comes forward to face* **Marie** *who rises from her chair.*

Marie   Dear Ma, I never though I'd be sick of the sun, but Perth has only so many beaches you can lie on. I miss you and I know things are bad because you haven't written. I've met a guy built like a Chippendale, even if conversation isn't his strong point. His whole family are the same, like the *Flintstones* with the sound turned off. They think I'm mad. I must be with what I'm after doing, but that will save for another day. Say hello to Dessie for me.

Dessie *rises and looks at* **Jane** *alone on the stage.*

Dessie I saw a picture in the papers of the derelict house in Dolphin's Barn where a girl's body was found. Dead for two days. The features sounded similar but after a while all junkies look the same.

Dessie *puts his arm around* **Jane** *and holds her as she steps forward.*

Jane I'm ready, officer, you can uncover the face. I've been here before, quite an expert on morgues. (*Long beat, softly*) Sweet Jesus, that's my daughter or what the drugs left of her.

Christy *and* **Carmel** *rise to stand in silent sympathy on the edge of the stage as* **Jane** *backs away, leaving* **Dessie** *to approach* **Marie** *who enters from the left.*

Dessie I collected Marie at the airport. Seemed like another life since I saw her off in Tomo's Triumph Herald.

They embrace.

Marie I should have been here for them.

Dessie It would have made no difference.

Marie (*breaks from embrace*) How's my mother?

Dessie I don't know how much is resignation and how much is Valium.

Marie Ballymun hasn't changed. Chips with everything and Valium with everything else.

Dessie It has changed. You'd hardly know a soul.

Marie (*tearful*) I should have come home for them both. But that's the thing with being an illegal emigrant. You can drift through the black economy forever provided you don't leave the country.

Dessie Does that mean you can't go back?

Marie I can go where I like. My status has changed. (*Beat*) Two months ago I got married.

Dessie You got what?

Marie It's eight years, Dessie. What did you expect me to do? Lock myself in the wardrobe with a vibrator and only leave the house for batteries?

Dessie You could have written and told me.

Marie You could have told me how bad Sharon was.

Dessie We were trying to let you get on with living your life.

Marie And I was trying to let you get on with yours.

(*Beat*) Easy knowing we're old friends, back together two minutes and we're fighting.

Dessie   There's no one I'd sooner fight with.

Marie   I missed you all. What sort of fool sits on a beach in Perth and misses Ballymun?

Dessie   I wouldn't know.

Marie   No. You get homesick while still at home.

Dessie   What's this husband like?

Marie   Bursting with hormones, great in the sack.

Dessie   Better than me.

Marie   I can't make comparisons, you never really lasted long enough.

Dessie   Thanks.

Marie   I'm slagging. Something I can't do with Greg. He's perpetually hurling his surfboard at the nearest wave to prove his endurance. Your version of endurance was wearing the same shirt for three weeks. He wanted to come, but I wanted to be able to focus on my ma, not spend the whole time explaining Ballymun to an outsider.

Christy *and* **Carmel** *step forward as if miming carrying a coffin on their shoulders, with* **Dessie** *and* **Marie** *falling in behind them. The image quickly dissolves as they stand in a row as if in church.*

Christy Sharon's coffin was light. Marie insisted on being a pallbearer, her and Dessie at the front, me and three other neighbours behind carrying it into the church of the Virgin Mary in Shangan. A small attendance of the old stock. Newcomers to the towers only really knew her from being robbed in her desperation. Other junkies hanging around at the back, knowing their turn would come. Pinpricks of eyes and faces like bog skeletons. (**Jane** *approaches* **Carmel** *and hands her a piece of paper.*) Jane found a poem Sharon wrote when she was twelve. My heart went crossways when I saw who was asked to read it aloud.

Carmel (*slowly from the piece of paper*)

> The stairs are dark and scary,
> But they lead up to the sky.
> Here in a nest of concrete
> Live my mum, my sister and I.
>
> The sun shines on the balcony
> And as each gull floats by
> I study their graceful wings
> So I can learn to fly.

During this poem **Sharon** *crosses the stage like a ghost, at ease, glancing back with affection as she says the last line softly along with* **Carmel**. *She exits and the others follow, leaving just* **Marie** *and* **Jane**.

Marie (*to* **Jane**)   I'm glad everyone's gone. Don't think I'll ever feel warm again. It's time you left here, Mum.

Jane   Since 1972 I've been dying to get away. I'd applied for the surrender grant, planned to rent a small flat for Sharon and me, somewhere in the city away from drugs.

Marie   It would have made no difference. She'd have still found her way out to here or Fatima Mansions.

Jane (*suddenly bitter*)   You weren't here, you don't know.

Marie   I know the pain you're in.

Jane   I shouldn't have said that. I never told you how bad she was because I didn't want your life ruined too.

Marie   You think I couldn't read between the lines? Come back to Australia with me.

Jane   What would I do there?

Marie   Live. Something you haven't done for years.

Jane I've lived all right, through emotions I never had names for. I've hunted for my child in dark places with other mothers, been threatened by knives, had my last possessions stolen by my own daughter. Yet I never stopped loving Sharon in a way that I have never loved you.

Marie (*upset*) Mum …

Jane It's true. Because you never needed me like she did. We went through things more intense than childbirth. She hated the Coolmines clinic. Four times we tried to detox here instead, journeying through hell together, not caring what screams the neighbours heard.

Marie Come back to Perth with me.

Jane As part of one big family? You couldn't even bring your mysterious husband home for your sister's funeral.

Marie I thought it would complicate things.

Jane For who? I can't blame you because you inherit your snobbery from me.

Marie It's not that.

Jane In your clean new life you don't want him to see where you came from. I was ashamed of my address for

85

years and it made me ashamed of myself. But I'm ashamed of nothing now.

Marie Maybe I'm like you, but not in the way you think. I fall for similar men.

Jane You fell for Dessie.

Marie Dessie didn't seem exciting enough. Three weeks after I married Greg I discovered he was still seeing someone, unfinished business with an old flame. I realised that I'd married my father.

Jane What did you do?

Marie What you should have done. I hit him.

Jane And what did he do?

Marie He hit me back, only harder. We're on round fifteen, every time the bell goes we try to knock each other out. That's why I didn't bring him.

Jane I can't go back with you. Not until they knock this tower down. Sharon's ghost haunts this flat, still needing me like you never will.

Marie *turns to face* **Dessie** *who enters. She leaves* **Jane** *to join him.* **Jane** *cuts an isolated figure on stage while* **Christy** *comes to stand at the back of the stage and listen.*

Dessie I should buy shares in this airport.

Marie You didn't have to come.

Dessie You wouldn't be an emigrant without somebody to forlornly wave you off.

Marie I'm not an emigrant any more, I'm an Australian. You could spread your wings, visit us, or would that be too much of a change?

Dessie I've changed a lot. I just didn't need to go half-way around the world to do so.

Marie People have a choice.

Dessie I respect yours, but that doesn't mean I've stood still. If I haven't physically travelled as far maybe that's because I'm on a different journey. I was born in a tenement to a da with copperplate handwriting. Neighbours would get him to write letters for them, imagining his penmanship would impress officials. It didn't because nobody listened to tenement dwellers. Now I sit at meetings as a full-time union official arguing people's cases and the bosses and officials have to listen. They think me a jumped up little bollix, but I make them nervous. When people were dumped out here in the 1960s nobody asked what we wanted: they made decisions for us. My journey is to make them listen. Not exciting, not glamorous, but I've travelled a long way from where Da started.

Marie   Maybe so, but there again what else have you known?

Dessie   I've known love, with you, every second of it precious.

Marie   That was a lifetime ago. For Christ's sake, we shouldn't be having this conversation. I'm a married woman battered around the edges.

Dessie   I loved you from day one. Since you left there were other women. I've tried to forget you but I can't bear seeing you get on that plane.

Marie   I've a new life, Dessie, and, for all your talk, your da's unemployed again. It's a bloody recession and young people are emigrating like in the 1950s. You see change here, but I don't. If you'd come with me eight years ago maybe it wouldn't have worked out but we could have bloody well tried.

Dessie *turns as* **Marie** *exits.*

Dessie   I got pissed in the airport after Marie left. She was right. Late 1980s Ballymun was on its last legs. The abandoned suburb. Still, at least the Ballymun Workmen's Club finally opened, eleven years behind schedule. (**Christy** *crosses the stage to sit at the front.*) Da had somewhere to go with others of his generation who would never see work again either. He bored them silly with his new obsession about lap times because, in Charlie, he was nurturing an Irish schoolboy champion swimmer.

Dessie *sits on the stage, watching his parents.*

Christy It's in the genes, you know. In my dancing days in the Metropole girls often commented on my resemblance to Johnny Weissmuller, the champion swimmer.

Carmel *approaches* **Christy.**

Carmel What rubbish are you spouting now?

Christy (*caught out*) What's that?

Carmel Were you telling the new tenants about some unfortunate girl mistaking you for Johnny Weissmuller fifty years ago?

Christy I was merely informing them about the medals young Charlie has won.

Carmel When I think of those poor girls you used to date from the Home for the Blind. You probably sat at a bus stop and claimed that you'd paid in for them to see the silent films. (*Sternly*) Have you Charlie's kit bag?

Christy   I have.

Carmel   His goggles?

Christy (*rises, annoyed, and exits*)   His snorkel, his knife to fight off marauding whales.

Carmel (*calls after him proudly before she exits in the opposite direction*)   Then hurry up. They have the pool open especially for him.

Dessie *turns his attention to* **Jane** *who has remained on stage.*

Jane   Grief is the greatest bushwacker of all, lurking in ambush at every corner. Finding things belonging to Sharon months after she died. The flat never seemed warm or maybe I was never warm. Dealers avoided my eye on the stairs, like they knew that there was nothing left they could do to me. I wasn't afraid of death and they were scared by my lack of fear. They left me alone. I thought the world would too, but it didn't. Through Carmel I'd met all kinds of neighbours who called by at odd moments and sat with me, saying the usual things or nothing at all. Then out of the blue the Community Coalition asked me to join the steering committee to start a Credit Union. It would be Ballymun's way to shaft the banks who'd shafted us. I explained that I was in grief but they knew about Sharon and said they respected all I'd been through. After they left I found myself shaking.

Respect. Such an odd word and so long since I'd heard anyone apply it to me.

Christy (*from his seat*) They asked me to join the steering committee too, but I'd enough to be doing training a future Olympic champion.

Jane *exits*.

Dessie Charlie was a flyer. Leinster schoolboy champion. Slaughtering kids from schools with their own pools. The *Ballymun News* printed a piece on the eve of a race to pick who would represent the Irish schools abroad. Da waffled on to the reporter about naming him after Charlie Haughey and how, since being wheeled in his pram down to his first protest, locals always asked Ma to bring Charlie along as a good-luck charm to every protest since. When the race happened didn't half of Ballymun turn up in Dublin jerseys, roaring their heads off, with posh parents shifting in their seats, terrified that their hubcaps were about to be stolen. Charlie won and 'Good Luck' banners hung from half the balconies in the tower block. The day before Charlie flew to London Da came in holding the post and looking like he needed a post to hold himself up with.

Christy *enters from the left, holding an envelope, looking shocked.* **Carmel** *enters from the right, worried by him.* **Dessie** *rises between them.*

Carmel What is it? A bill?

Christy (*awestruck*) A letter ... from him.

Carmel From who?

Christy Charlie.

Carmel Sure isn't Charlie inside watching telly?

Christy (*trembling*) Charlie Haughey. From Charlie to Charlie. (*Roars*) Charlie, get out here, your Taoiseach has written to you! (*To* **Carmel**) You read this.

Carmel I can't read.

Christy You can so.

Carmel I've forgotten.

Christy (*handing it to* **Dessie**) Here, Dessie, be careful opening it in case there's a big cheque and a nought slips off.

Dessie (*opening it*) '*Office of the Taoiseach. Dear Charlie, Good luck with your race for Ireland. Yours sincerely, Charles J. Haughey, Taoiseach. P.S. Mind them English girls.*'

Christy (*delighted, exiting*) Good old Charlie, he never forgets his own.

Dessie   Da had it framed. Said it beat a cheque any day because you'd have to cash a cheque whereas you keep this to show to your grandchildren.

Dessie *follows* **Christy** *off, leaving* **Carmel** *alone.*

Carmel   Devil the sign of grandchildren. Not that girls weren't fond of Dessie. Twice he moved in with one, an apartment in Phibsborough, another in Donnybrook. The second girl already had a child. It seemed I'd be a granny by proxy, but Dessie was too picky or his heart wasn't fully in it. He'd move back in here, said he missed kicking football with Charlie and arguing with his da. I think he missed the flats and being involved in helping to run everything. Because, being a good talker, he got roped onto every deputation. And you know, finally there was a sense of officials considering our views. Dessie's dream was simple. Start from scratch. Don't break up the community but firstly build new homes and shops and then knock the old towers down. I just wish he'd bought himself a house somewhere before prices rocketed. Still I was glad of his few bob with Christy out of work and Charlie to be fed. I managed well, borrowing if necessary – not from loan sharks this time. Instead sitting up in the Credit Union with Jane, working out figures as one Ballymuner to another. Such a long way from sitting in her kitchen struggling to read *The Cat in the Hat*. Jane virtually ran the Credit Union, yet her eyes never lost their haunted look.

Jane *has risen to stand on the opposite side of the stage.* **Carmel** *now exits.*

Jane It was towards dusk on a winter Tuesday. Her footsteps on the stairwell so slight that I don't know why they disturbed me. (*The* **Junkie** *crosses the stage in front of her, furtively, scared, suicidal.*) I opened the door on the chain, barely glimpsed her face as she passed, but something about it … the pinprick eyes, the bones protruding. (**Jane** *follows the girl*) I followed and she knew I was following and ran to get away. I knew where she was headed, the abandoned flat above me with its door forced open, access to a balcony. Her footsteps were slow like her limbs no longer did what they were told.

The **Junkie** *stops on the edge of the stage, hunched up, hands rubbing her shoulders for comfort, and looks back.*

Junkie What do you want, bitch?

Jane Please, step back from the edge.

Junkie Shove off, leave me alone.

Jane Please, I want to help.

Junkie If you want to help then just fuck off. What would you know?

Jane More than you think.

Junkie (*Quieter*) I'm doing no harm here, missus. Just want to be alone.

Jane I know about being alone too. I've whiskey in my flat, Valium the doctor prescribed once. I've food if …

Junkie (*Jittery*) Are you fucking deaf? I want to be alone.

Jane *Cautiously approaching*) It's a long fall. You think it will be easy, but it won't. I've stood on a balcony. After a time the ground starts to move. You can't go forward and can't go back. You're stuck there like a fly on insect paper.

Junkie Will you shut up?

Jane I won't. I lost a daughter your age to heroin. Maybe there was nothing I could have done, but that doesn't stop me lying awake questioning myself. Things have changed here. There is help like there wasn't before, a methadone van quietly parked by the road. It's difficult but you can get through this.

Junkie My ma threw me out, said she was sick of me stealing everything.

Jane I know. I called my daughter every name.

Junkie You don't know. You're not my ma.

Jane There's a bed downstairs not slept in for years. I've been through cold turkey with her. Maybe this time ... maybe I'm a junkie too, strung out on hope.

Junkie You got any smokes?

Jane Downstairs.

Junkie Ice-cream?

Jane (*Holds out a hand*) Just take my hand.

Junkie Keep away or I'll jump.

Jane You won't. Only boys jump, girls fall. You don't want to die.

Junkie I've no reason to live.

Jane You've a whole life ahead of you.

Junkie To end up like you, is it, a lonely old bitch? (*Shivers*) I need something.

Jane Cigarettes, Valium, downstairs. We can walk to the clinic.

Junkie You got money down there?

Jane (*steps forward, grips her shoulders*)   Listen to me, it will be okay.

Junkie (*freaks*)   Don't touch me! Don't hit! I'm sick of people hitting. Just want to be held …

Jane (*calming her*)   Just step away from the edge.

Junkie   Leave me alone! (*Blindly she pushes Jane away, then reaches out desperately as Jane staggers forward*) God, I didn't mean to push, Christ help me. Valium, cigarettes, got to get …

The **Junkie** *turns away to sit on the back of the stage, leaving* **Jane** *alone, standing utterly still.*

Jane   And I was gone, through the broken bars of the balcony, my last thought to curse her and curse myself and then my brain froze … the terrible sense of falling. Then my terror was gone and I was looking down from a height at how I had landed, how old my face looked. The gathering adults pushing children back. The dark tarmac, the blood, stress lines on faces. I was beyond it all at this green height, calmly detached. I wanted to watch but something pulled me on, beyond Balbutcher and Balcurris, towards a landscape I didn't know. (**Sharon** *enters the stage behind* **Jane**.) I wondered where Sharon was, would she be waiting and if the next tenant in my flat would feel an unexplained coldness. (**Sharon** *takes her* *hand and leads her gently to the back of the stage*) But maybe the coldness would be gone and Sharon and I could start again as equals and sisters.

Christy *and* **Carmel** *enter from the right with* **Dessie**.

Christy   Another funeral and no one could explain why Jane jumped after all this time. If only walls could speak … and God knows the walls around here could tell enough.

Marie *enters from the left and* **Dessie** *goes to join her, watched by all the others.*

Dessie   I didn't know if you'd still be here.

Marie   Someone has to clear out the flat.

Dessie   Your husband didn't come.

Marie   I was always asking her to visit Australia, for six months even. What was she doing, rotting away here?

Dessie (*Takes a step closer*)   Marie.

Marie (*panics*)   Don't touch me, sick of people hitting … just want to be held …

Dessie (*embraces her*)   Who hit you?

Marie   No one.

Dessie   I'll get on a plane and rip his heart out.

Marie   It's over, I left him. I used to write to Mum and pretend the marriage was okay. I wanted her to think one of us was happy.

Dessie   Don't go back.

Marie   What?

Dessie   Marry me or live with me or do whatever you want with me.

Marie   I've a good life in Australia, an apartment, a job.

Dessie   A man?

Marie   A recent history of one-night mistakes.

Dessie   Stay. I want you with me.

Marie   You don't know me any more, Dessie. I'm thirty-four and I feel like fifty.

Dessie   You could make me Australian shark steaks and I could make you laugh.

Marie   What would I live on?

Dessie Hope. There are jobs now, people returning all the time. They're going to knock down Ballymun, brick by brick, start all over again. We could do the same.

Marie They'd probably make a total balls of it the second time around too.

Dessie Maybe they will. The only way to find out is to stick around. It looks impressive on the plans.

Marie It always does. Who wants to live on a building site for the next ten years?

Dessie I'll buy you wellingtons. I could fancy you in wellingtons.

Marie I'm trouble, Dessie, I fly off the handle. Inside a week we won't be talking.

Dessie And inside another week we will.

Marie I've already bought a return ticket.

Dessie Use it any time you like. Stay with me. Let's watch them build the future, it will be great.

Marie Why, because it looks good on the plans?

Dessie No, because you'll be going to share it with me.

Marie (*long beat, then embraces him*) Holy God, I must be cracked.

Christy They never bothered with a wedding. I wouldn't mind only I'd a great speech in my head. They moved into Jane's flat. Over the mantelpiece they put a framed unused return ticket to Australia and a sign Dessie stole from a hotel – 'In case of emergency break the glass'. (*Looks at* **Carmel** *beside him, smiling, holding a glasses case*) Carmel and me knocked along until cancer got her three years ago. We buried her in Dardistown, hands clasped around her reading glasses. She was always losing them when wanting to do the crossword. I kept losing everything in that empty flat after she died, even when Dessie and Marie and my darling granddaughter moved in to keep me company. (*Tara has entered to stand beside her parents, all watching* **Christy**.) I've two more grandchildren in America where Charlie teaches physical education. He went over on an athletics scholarship and married an African runner, a beauty. He thought I'd mind. Listen, Charlie, says I, as long as she's not from Cork.

Dessie Last year Da insisted on moving himself into a flat in the old folks' complex where he knows everyone. Said he didn't want to be here when they knock the tower down. We visit him four times a week. Tara and him are thick as thieves, with her believing all his tales. He gets confused at times but that's to be expected. Still he's happy, even if he keeps complaining that he'd love a few pigeons.

Tara   And my new home is ready to move into after we finished packing here. That's where we'll be going any time now once Ma lets a good shout at Dad to stop him day-dreaming. I had a dream last night. I didn't know the people in it but I knew that one was my Aunt Sharon who's dead because people say I look like her. There were all kinds of people passing on the main road in a silent procession. People going one way and more going the other and they had suitcases and old prams with televisions in them and pillow cases stuffed with clothes and no one seemed able to see each other. Still it wasn't scary. I was waving from the balcony but they were too busy getting on with their lives, I suppose, and I was too excited about my big move to really pay them much attention. You see, I still have my teddies to pack and soon I'll have to take Daddy's hand and lead him out the door here because I'm dying to see my new bedroom and close the door and arrange all my posters and teddies and then I'll be able to call it home.

Fade to blackout.

Ballymun Incantation

Whose voice can you hear?
Who's calling down the stair?
What ghost trapped in a lift shaft?
What child who played and laughed?

In nineteen hundred and sixty seven,
Craning our necks towards heaven,
We arrived here by truck and bus,
Three thousand families of us.

Tea chests and cardboard suitcases,
Boxes bound with old shoelaces,
From tenements in condemned streets,
Now the world appeared at our feet.

Crowding the lifts and up each stair,
Onto the balconies to breathe the air,
We were so dizzy all Dublin spun:
The chosen families of Ballymun.

I think this heat is killing us.
Why can't we turn off the radiators?
Where are the shops we were promised?
Why won't they come to fix the broken lifts?

My name is Mary, when I turned nine
I slept alone for the first time,
My sister whispering secrets overhead
In Ceannt Tower in a new bunk bed.

In Plunkett Tower my wife grew shook,
She was alone when the lift got stuck,

She hated the squatters jarring her nerves,
I still see her shaking, reciting prayers.

My name is Agnes, when I was born,
The Civil War was still raging on.
I moved to Balcurris with my grandchildren,
I lived for Novenas and Sweet Afton.

My name is John, I stole my first kiss
Just before the doors opened in the lift.
Eilish was still in her school uniform,
Surely no other love could be this strong.

Help me, I'm still lost here and all alone,
I injected my mother's hopes into my arm,
Shivering in the depths of cold turkey
I thought I could fly from this balcony.

Why won't the voices stop whispering,
Straining to be heard amid the babbling?
Lives that were ended and lives begun,
The living and the dead of Ballymun.

Remember my name, it is Elizabeth,
In the local workhouse I faced my death.
Cholera stole away my famished son,
I buried him amid the fields of Ballymun.

Remember me, my ghost also haunts here,
Seeking my child who fell through the air.
The coroner declared my death was suicide,
I just wanted to be my dead daughter's side.

I loved the marches during the rent strikes,
All us boys riding behind on chopper bikes,
It was brilliant there laughing with my mates,
That's where I asked Joan for our first date.

Every touch and every thrust and every kiss
Every feud, every fight, every lip split,
Every face lost at the window of a tower block
Every loan shark with a list of women in hock.

Every whiskey, every Valium, every cigarette,
Every couple holding hands in a kitchenette,
Every laughing child being spun in the August sun
Every boy with a piebald horse to gallop on.

Every mother dreaming about some different life,
Every first tooth, first communion, every surgeon's knife,
Every welder, office cleaner, every unemployed,
Every girl who fought back when her dreams died.

Every young poet who wrote it out in verse:
McDonagh and Mac Dermott, Connolly and Pearse,
Every name scrawled on walls in each tower block,
Every face that is remembered, every face forgot,

Every life that ended here and every life begun:
The living and the dead of Ballymun.

Dermot Bolger

'Ballymun Incantation' was composed by the author to be recited
by actors and local people as the centrepiece of a public wake on
the eve of the demolition of the first Ballymun tower in the summer
of 2004.

By the same author

Plays:
The Lament for Arthur Cleary
Blinded by the Light
In High Germany
The Holy Ground
One Last White Horse
April Bright
The Passion of Jerome
Consenting Adults

Stage adaptations:
A Dublin Bloom
(a free adaptation of James Joyce's *Ulysses*)

Novels:
Night Shift
The Woman's Daughter
The Journey Home
Emily's Shoes
A Second Life
Father's Music
Temptation
The Valparaiso Voyage
The Family on Paradise Pier

Poetry:
The Habit of Flesh
Finglas Lilies
No Waiting America
Internal Exiles
Leinster Street Ghosts
Taking My Letters Back: New and Selected Poems
The Chosen Moment